HATE SPEECH

The MIT Press Essential Knowledge Series

A complete list of the titles in this series appears at the back of this book.

HATE SPEECH

CAITLIN RING CARLSON

The MIT Press | Cambridge, Massachusetts | London, England

This book was set in Chaparral Pro by New Best-set Typesetters Ltd. Printed and bound in the United States of America.

Library of Congress Cataloging-in-Publication Data

Names: Carlson, Caitlin Ring, author.
Title: Hate speech / Caitlin Ring Carlson.
Description: Cambridge, Massachusetts The MIT Press, 2021. | Series: The MIT Press essential knowledge series | Includes bibliographical references and index.
Identifiers: LCCN 2020004631 | ISBN 9780262539906 (paperback)
Subjects: LCSH: Hate speech—Law and legislation. | Hate speech—Law and legislation—United States. | Hate speech. | Hate speech—United States.
Classification: LCC K5210 .C37 2021 | DDC 342.08/53—dc23
LC record available at https://lccn.loc.gov/2020004631

10 9 8 7 6 5 4 3 2 1

CONTENTS

SERIES FOREWORD

The MIT Press Essential Knowledge series offers accessible, concise, beautifully produced pocket-size books on topics of current interest. Written by leading thinkers, the books in this series deliver expert overviews of subjects that range from the cultural and the historical to the scientific and the technical.

In today's era of instant information gratification, we have ready access to opinions, rationalizations, and superficial descriptions. Much harder to come by is the foundational knowledge that informs a principled understanding of the world. Essential Knowledge books fill that need. Synthesizing specialized subject matter for nonspecialists and engaging critical topics through fundamentals, each of these compact volumes offers readers a point of access to complex ideas.

INTRODUCTION

In Virginia, young men in khaki pants and white polo shirts march through the center of a public university campus, shouting "Jews will not replace us." In the Tsuruhashi district of Osaka, Japan, a 14-year-old girl addresses the crowd, saying how much she despises Korean people and wishes she could kill them all. In Myanmar, a Facebook user publishes a post to his page about Bengalis, calling them dogs who are destroying his land and his people. In Cape Town, a pastor makes a comment online asking ISIS to "please come rid South Africa of the homosexual curse."

Unfortunately, no culture, country, or form of communication is immune from the existence or influence of hate speech. Whether online or in person, people wield language as a weapon to attack one another's identities, reaffirming their own perceived position of dominance and solidifying their feelings of belonging to a given social group. The impact of this expression is detrimental, both to the individuals targeted and to the societies that condone its use. Hate speech traumatizes its victims and negatively impacts their self-worth; it silences political participation and distorts public discourse. Hate speech can also be used as a tool to dehumanize groups, normalizing violence against them by amplifying egregious claims through mass media. Despite the problems it causes, cultural and political policy makers continue to struggle with regulating hate speech.

Defining Hate Speech

Hate speech is an expansive and contested term. Part of what is so challenging about this issue is the fact that scholars don't agree on what hate speech is, or is not. The Anti-Defamation League's former national director, Abraham H. Foxman, and attorney Christopher Wolf argue that hate speech includes broad categories of speech, including racism, anti-Semitism, homophobia, bigotry against the disabled, political hatred, rumormongering, misogyny and violent pornography, promotion of terrorism, cyberbullying, harassment, stalking, and the sale and promotion of online products.[1] In an effort to regulate this type of expression, many countries have legally defined hate speech. The European Union's "Framework Decision on Combating

No culture, country, or form of communication is immune from the existence or influence of hate speech.

Certain Forms and Expressions of Racism and Xenophobia by Means of Criminal Law" defines hate speech as "public incitement to violence or hatred directed to groups or individuals on the basis of certain characteristics, including race, color, religion, descent, and national or ethnic origin." Notably, the EU does not include gender, sexual orientation, gender identity, age, or disability on this list.[2] Broadly, hate speech should be defined as expression that seeks to malign an individual for their immutable characteristics, such as their race, ethnicity, national origin, religion, gender, gender identity, sexual orientation, age, or disability. I use the term "expression" because hate speech includes not only spoken words, but also symbols and images that degrade people for the qualities they're born with.

Each conception of hate speech presented here talks about it as being a form of expression that degrades a person based on their fixed characteristics. However, after reading Kate Manne's *Down Girl*, I consider hate speech to be a structural issue. In her book, Manne reconceptualizes the definition of misogyny. Rather than a deep-seated hatred of women by men, as many long thought, misogyny is recast as a structural phenomenon that works to control, police, and punish women who subvert the existing system of male dominance.[3] For example, when Hillary Clinton received the Democratic Party's nomination for President of the United States in 2016, supporters of her opponent, Donald Trump, shouted "Lock the bitch up" at his political rallies. At the Republican National Convention, vendors sold T-shirts that read "Trump that bitch" and "If you can read this, the bitch fell off." Like a game of whack-a-mole, misogyny works to hammer down women who threaten men's social, economic, or political dominance.

Like Manne's definition of misogyny, hate speech represents a structural phenomenon in which those in power use verbal assaults and offensive imagery to maintain their preferred position in the existing social order. In the United States, White people have long used the N-word or called an African American man "boy" to reinforce White supremacy. In Japan, an extremist organization, Zaitoku-kai, believes Zainichi Koreans have unearned, special privileges in Japanese society. Terms like "cockroaches" and "criminals" are used to diminish the humanity of Zainichi Koreans and the Zaitokukai openly call for their massacre. By putting others down, the Zaitokukai expose themselves as a threatened class attempting to maintain their position of dominance in the social structure.

In addition to clarifying what hate speech is, it is also important to understand what it is not. Hate speech is not synonymous with offensive speech. Words or images that someone finds upsetting or hurtful do not meet legal or even colloquial definitions of hate speech. Saying that you don't like someone, their personality or their politics, does not constitute hate speech. In order to be considered hate speech, expression must directly attack a person's

Hate speech represents a structural phenomenon in which those in power use verbal assaults and offensive imagery to maintain their preferred position in the existing social order.

immutable identity characteristics such as race, gender, or sexual orientation.

Hate speech also differs from hate crimes. Hate crimes are criminal acts that are motivated by prejudice against a victim or victims because of their immutable characteristics, such as their race, religion, or ethnicity. If a criminal act is designated as a hate crime, it often carries additional penalties such as an increased prison sentence. Hate speech may be used during the commission of a hate crime but the terms are not synonymous with one another.

The Continuum of Hate

The Anti-Defamation League (ADL) released the Pyramid of Hate in 2018, which breaks down how certain behaviors can form the foundation for bias-motivated violence. At the base of the pyramid are biased attitudes, which include or are evident in stereotyping, insensitive remarks, fear of difference, non-inclusive language, and microaggressions. Building on top of biased attitudes, acts of bias encompass bullying, ridicule, slurs/epithets, dehumanization, or biased or belittling jokes. The next level of the pyramid is discrimination, which comes in various forms including economic discrimination, educational discrimination, criminal discrimination, and segregation.

The second highest level of the pyramid is bias-motivated violence, which includes all manner of hate

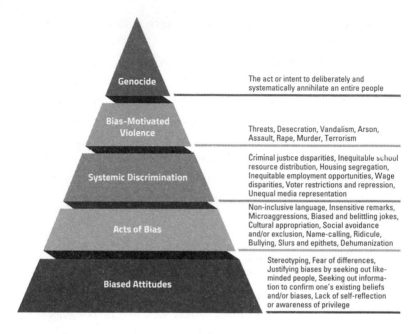

Figure 1 The Anti-Defamation League's Pyramid of Hate illustrates the prevalence of bias, hate, and oppression in society. It is organized in escalating levels of attitudes and behavior that grow in complexity from bottom to top. © 2019 Anti-Defamation League, www.adl.org. Reprinted with permission.

crimes, from assault to arson to rape and even murder. At the pinnacle of the pyramid is genocide, which refers to the systematic annihilation of a group of people.

The ADL intentionally selected a pyramid to represent how hate progresses along a continuum. Verbal transgressions such as stereotypes and ethnic slurs become the bedrock upon which discrimination or genocide is built: "The very purpose of intimidating hate speech is to perpetuate and augment existing inequalities. Although the spread of intimidating hate speech does not *always* lead to the commission of discriminatory violence, it establishes the rationale for attacking particular disfavored groups."[4]

The pyramid clarifies that hate speech is foundational to problems such as discrimination, bias-motivated violence, and genocide. If the behaviors on the lower levels of the pyramid are treated as normal, the next level becomes more acceptable among both individuals and institutions. Rather than viewing hate speech as a symptom of racism or sexism, hate speech should be viewed as a driving force for these issues. The casual use of hate speech leads to the behaviors at the top of the pyramid, which have life-threatening consequences.

Hate Speech and Freedom of Expression

While hate speech can and does cause very real harm, silencing people before their ideas have had a chance to be considered also raises serious concerns. For centuries, scholars and philosophers have been wrestling with questions about the dangers of censorship by governments and other institutions. One of the most widely cited justifications for allowing all expression, including hate speech, is known as the marketplace of ideas. This theory suggests that in order for truth to be found, all ideas, even bad ones, must be thrown into competition with one another so that the best among them may emerge. Therefore, no idea should be silenced before it has had a chance to be heard.

The notion of the marketplace of ideas dates back to John Milton's 1644 work, *Areopagitica*, which condemned an order from the English Parliament to regulate book printing. Truth, Milton said, should be permitted to grapple with falsehood, knowing that in the end, truth would emerge victorious from the debate.[5]

In his 1859 book, *On Liberty*, John Stuart Mill said that human ideas and opinions prove themselves only when they are challenged over time. Mill's work laid much of the foundation for the liberal democratic tradition, which defends the public's right to hear and to speak freely as a necessary component of enlightenment. Humanity will be better off, said Mill, when truth is left to compete with error in the open market.[6] Therefore, every individual should be granted the opportunity to share their opinions and ideas so that, ideally, the best among them will emerge. Mill recognized, however, that truth may not always triumph. After all, history teems with examples in which truth has been put down by persecution.

The notion of the marketplace of ideas was introduced to US jurisprudence by Justice Oliver Wendell Holmes, who famously used the concept in his dissent in the case *Abrams v. United States* (1919), which upheld the conviction of a man for distributing leaflets denouncing the war and the plan to send American troops to Russia. Here, Holmes argued that the ultimate good that we all desire is better reached by free trade in ideas, rather than their suppression. The best test of truth, said Justice Holmes, "is the power of the thought to get itself accepted in the competition of the market."[7] Unlike Mill's approach, Justice Holmes's test for truth was not only concerned with objective truth, but also the will of the majority.

In the United States, there are only a handful of instances when it is permissible for the government to silence expression before it has had a chance to reach the marketplace. These exceptions come from a 1931 Supreme Court case called *Near v. Minnesota*, which involved the censorship of a Minneapolis newspaper run by Jay Near. In several issues, Near asserted that Jews were "practically ruling" the city, that the chief of police was taking bribes, and that the governor was incompetent. Near was prevented from publishing his newspaper in 1925 on the grounds that it violated a public nuisance law, which said that anyone regularly publishing or circulating an "obscene, lewd, and lascivious" or a "malicious, scandalous, and defamatory" newspaper or periodical was guilty of a nuisance, and could be enjoined from further committing or maintaining the nuisance.[8] Near challenged the state's decision to shut down his paper. Upon hearing the case, the Supreme Court found the law to be a violation of the free press clause of the First Amendment, and established the doctrine that, with some narrow exceptions, the government could not censor or prohibit publication in advance, even if the content in question might be punishable after publication. Today, these exceptions include threats to national security, efforts to overthrow the government, impediments to military recruitment, incitements to violence, fighting words, and obscenity. Notably, hate speech is not included on this list.

Along with the marketplace of ideas, another often-cited reason for protecting all speech, including hate speech, is the importance of free expression in the democratic process. This theory, which originated from John Locke's political philosophy and was popularized by Alexander Meiklejohn in the middle of the twentieth century, suggests that in a democracy, all expression must be permitted so that citizens have access to the information they need to govern themselves effectively.[9] Rather than having rules imposed from on high, citizens in a representative democracy enter into a social contract with one another. We elect members of our community to make decisions on our behalf. In order for this process of making and remaking decisions to be effective, we need access to all available information. People, Meiklejohn said, should be able to freely discuss, praise, or criticize government policies and practices in order to carry out their civic duty. Robust and open public debate is essential to achieving our shared social or democratic goals. Therefore, we must protect all expression, including hate speech, in order to achieve our democratic ideals.

In addition to the societal aims outlined by the marketplace of ideas and political self-governance theories, personal liberty is another important reason to protect even the most vile expression. This theory, which can be traced back to Thomas I. Emerson, suggests that we should not curtail hateful or bigoted speech because every human being deserves the right to express herself or himself fully.[10] Infringing on this right infringes on our personal liberty, which is essential to achieving our full human potential.

While the dangers of allowing hate speech to spread within a society are evident, so too are the concerns associated with silencing any kind of expression before it has had a chance to reach the marketplace. Questions regarding the legal regulation of hate speech also raise concerns about how the term will be defined and by whom. Giving governments the power to potentially label expression they dislike as hate speech puts them in a position to suppress opposing ideas. This fear, along with a desire to protect the marketplace of ideas and the democratic process, is at least part of the reason that the United States chooses to protect hate speech while many other countries seek to legally prohibit it. Many of the nations with the strictest hate speech laws, such as Germany or South Africa, have experienced firsthand the role language plays in fueling bias-motivated violence. Before exploring how individual countries and cultures address the problem of hate speech, it is important to first understand the history of this phenomenon.

History of Hate Speech

Scholar Alexander Tsesis characterizes hate speech as the proverbial bark that comes before the bite of bias-motivated violence or genocide. Hate speech relies on stereotypes about insular groups to influence hostile behavior toward them. In his 2002 book, *Destructive Messages*, Tsesis describes how "misethnic discourses" were used to justify the American slave trade and the relocation of Native Americans.[11] Misethnic discourses include the practice of ascribing undesirable traits to members of these groups (for example, Native Americans are lazy) and using dehumanizing terms to describe these individuals. The list of offensive slurs used to characterize Africans, and eventually African Americans, is extensive. By depicting the objects of their hatred as sub-human or animal-like (for example, as "apes," "coons," or "monkeys"), Whites' violence against members of this group became normal and often expected.

Mass media and communication technologies have also shaped the use and impact of hate speech. After the Industrial Revolution, railways delivered newspapers and magazines widely, often spreading negative sentiments and misinformation about members of different identity groups to literate members of the population. In Nazi Germany, newspapers and radio disseminated propaganda against Jewish people, helping set the conditions for the Holocaust. In the late twentieth century, the Hutu ethnic majority in Rwanda used radio to spread misinformation about the Tutsis, resulting in the death of over eight hundred thousand people. Today, anyone can publish content with global reach on the internet and social media. Currently, military leaders and regular citizens in Myanmar use Facebook to spread a campaign of hate against the Rohingya and other Muslims, which has led to violence against these marginalized communities. By exploring each of these instances in greater detail, we can see how the creation, distribution, and impact of hate speech has (and hasn't) changed over time.

Case Studies

Germany
Before even one of the six million Jewish people who were murdered during the Holocaust were harmed, the

Nazi Party convinced German citizens that their deaths—along with the deaths of millions of Russians and Poles and thousands of Serbs, Romani, Black Germans, disabled people, and gay men and lesbians—were necessary. It begs the question, how do you convince a population to systematically kill that many people?

Tension has existed between Christians and Jewish people since the Middle Ages. Christians blamed the Jewish people for the death of Christ and expelled them from their communities after accusing them of blood libel (using the blood of Christians in religious rituals). When the German Empire emerged in the late nineteenth century, so too did the "Völkisch" movement. Loosely translated as "ethnic group," the movement was not necessarily a unified group, but a collection of beliefs about the racial superiority of Aryans. Leaders of this movement convinced the public that Aryans and Jewish people were in competition for world domination. Unsurprisingly, German folklore from the time regarded Jewish people as "vermin" or "rats," unworthy of life.

Anti-Semitism spread after Germany's defeat in World War I. In the years leading up to the Holocaust, German propaganda (in the form of both spoken/written words and images) argued that Jewish people were responsible for the loss of the war and were the driving force behind the economic hardships that Germany faced. The "Jew next door" became a threat, and ridding society of the racially "undesirable" became a reasonable response to Germany's problems. An offshoot of the Völkisch movement in the 1920s, the National Socialist German Workers Party painted "Jewry" as responsible for a host of problems faced by average citizens. Over the course of the next 25 years, the Nazis spread their extreme and radical views, creating a broad anti-Semitic consensus among the public throughout mass media.

Through highbrow editorials, letters to the editor, cartoons, and even children's books, Nazi propagandist Joseph Goebbels helped convince Germans that they would perish if something was not done to address the "Jewish Problem." Goebbels' own paper, *Der Angriff*, and the official newspaper of the National Socialist German Workers Party, *Völkischer Beobacter*, functioned as instruments of official propaganda from 1920–1945. Julius Streicher's *Der Stürmer* (published between 1923 and 1945) proved perhaps even more influential. Aimed at the man on the street, this publication featured letters from readers asking for assistance or complaining about Jewish people spreading rumors about them or engaging in unethical business dealings. Caricatures of Jewish people featured in cartoons drawn by Philip Rupprecht, whose pen name was "Fips," also proved popular. In these illustrations, Jewish people are depicted as short, fat, unshaven men and women with pig-like eyes who engage in unspeakable acts, such as killing children and drinking their blood. At the

Figure 2 Philip Rupprecht cartoon from March 1935, entitled "Don't Let Go!"
TRANSLATION:

> Do not grow weary, do not loosen the grip
> This poisonous serpent may not slip away
> Better that one strangles it to death
> Than that our misery begin anew

bottom of each page of the newspaper was the phrase "Die Juden dind unser Ungluck" — "Jews are our misfortune."

In addition to *Der Stürmer*, Julius Streicher also published a children's book written by his second in command at the paper, Ernst Hiemer. The eleven stories in the book compared Jewish people to various unpleasant animals, such as poisonous snakes and tapeworms:

> The Jew plays a similar role in the peoples he has entered. He is a freeloader, a parasite. Just as a tapeworm robs people of valuable nutrients, the Jew robs his host people of the best that they have. Farmers, the foundation of a healthy people, are sucked dry and destroyed by Jewish livestock traders. The Jew seizes a people's commerce and industry. A people's morality is undermined and its youth systematically corrupted. The people gradually sickens. The Jew takes its whole wealth and life force. If a people does not succeed in getting rid of the Jewish tapeworm in good time, it will be ruined.[12]

As is evident in this example, hate speech includes slurs and dehumanizing terms (vermin, snakes), as well as misethnic discourse, or attributing unfavorable traits to groups of people. Using language to liken members of a different race or ethnicity to animals or setting up an "us versus them" rhetorical dichotomy normalizes the mistreatment and violence toward members of those groups.

Rwanda

Like Germany, Rwanda has also experienced ethnic violence fueled by hate speech. During the 1990s, the Hutus disseminated hate speech about the Tutsis via radio and newspapers, emboldening regular citizens and militia members to engage in mass killings that resulted in five hundred thousand to one million civilian deaths, and reduced the country's Tutsi population by 75 percent.

The roots of this atrocity can be traced back to the time of colonial rule, when Belgians favored the minority Tutsis over the Hutus, creating the conditions for the oppression of many by an elite few. In 1959, the Hutus began killing Tutsis, forcing the emigration of over three hundred thousand people into neighboring nations. Years later, in 1990, Tutsi refugees, under the banner of the Rwandan Patriotic Front (RPF), invaded Rwanda from Uganda. The RPF and the Rwandan government reached a ceasefire, which held until 1994, when President Habyarimana's plane was shot down over the capital city of Kigali. This event ignited the flame between the two groups that had been endlessly stoked by mass media outlets over the preceding months.

Until the 1980s, Rwanda's state-run media consisted of two newspapers and one radio station, Radio Rwanda. In 1987, *Kangura* magazine emerged as an extreme and provocative voice.[13] In 1990, the magazine published its "Ten Commandments of the Hutu," describing the Tutsis as bloodthirsty traitors who were dishonest in business and sought the dominance of their ethnic group. However, newspapers were expensive to print and difficult to distribute, and literacy rates in the country were low. Radio, on the other hand, had enormous reach and could be disseminated to even the most rural villages in the country.

In 1993, President Habyarimana bankrolled Radio Télévision Libre des Mille Collines (RTLM). Top officials in the Rwandan government often played an active role at the station, determining the content of broadcasts, writing editorials, and giving journalists scripts to read.[14] The station's content was fairly moderate to start, which helped it build a substantial following, but it quickly became an electronic equivalent to *Kangura*, broadcasting popular music alongside racist propaganda. After President Habyarimana's plane was shot down, RTLM encouraged people to "exterminate" the Tutsi "injenzi" (cockroaches).

Much like Jewish people in Germany before the Holocaust, the Tutsis were framed as oppressors. RTLM broadcasts claimed that preemptive violence against the Tutsi ethnic group was necessary for self-defense and the only way to disrupt the historical cycle of discrimination. In her content analysis of taped RTLM broadcasts, scholar Mary Kimani found that these inflammatory broadcasts included reports of Tutsi RPF rebel atrocities, allegations that Tutsis were involved in a conspiracy against the Hutus, and allegations that the RPF wanted to take control of the Hutus and wield power over them.[15] Throughout all these broadcasts, government officials "instigated a limited number of acts of violence, catalyzed some key actors, coordinated elites, and bolstered local messages of violence."[16]

Taking a quantitative approach, scholar David Yanagizawa-Drott estimated the impact of RTLM broadcasts on the violence through a village-level data set.[17] He found that behavior in villages with reception was different than in those without. Yanagizawa-Drott estimated that over 10 percent of the overall violence (committed by fifty-one thousand perpetrators, including both militia groups and ordinary civilians) could be attributed to the station. Yanagizawa-Drott's work demonstrates how dehumanizing language can serve as a catalyst for violence against members of a particular ethnic group.

Myanmar

Muslims in Myanmar have faced discrimination within the predominantly Buddhist country for decades. However, recent violence toward members of this group, including rape, murder, and arson, has sparked the exodus of over seven hundred thousand Rohingya from Myanmar since 2017. For several years, Myanmar's military forces engaged in a campaign of propaganda promoting ethnic cleansing of the Rohingya. Unlike in Rwanda, where radio was used to spread hatred, Myanmar's military personnel have used Facebook to target the Rohingya. Military personnel used their own pages and created fake news accounts to post content portraying Rohingya as terrorists planning imminent jihadist attacks against Buddhists in the country. Like in Germany and Rwanda, the group waging the campaign of hatred and violence used a combination of dehumanizing terms and an "us or them" dichotomy to convince militia members and regular citizens that violence against this group was necessary for self-preservation.

After learning of the abuse, Facebook eventually removed the pages of many of Myanmar's military personnel. However, the company could not effectively regulate the imposter sites featuring Burmese pop stars, fake celebrity pages, and news sites. According to a 2018 Reuters investigation done in conjunction with the Human Rights Center and the University of California, Berkeley School of Law, these pages produced over one thousand posts calling Rohingya or other Muslims dogs, maggots, and rapists.[18] The posts, which are believed to be the work of over seven hundred military personnel, garnered 1.3 million followers by including direct calls to incite violence against the Rohingya.

One post read:

> These non-human kalar dogs, the Bengalis, are killing and destroying our land, our water, and our ethnic people. We need to destroy this race.

Another said:

> We must fight them the way hitler did the jews.
> Damn kalars.

Facebook, which relies heavily on users to report hate speech on its platform, responded slowly to this issue. In 2015, the company employed only four content moderators who spoke Burmese. Today, Accenture, the group that Facebook outsources parts of its content moderation to, employs 60 people to make decisions about hate speech and other content reported by Myanmar's eighteen million users.

Although these three case studies took place over the course of almost 100 years, the common thread that runs throughout each is the use of dehumanizing language to characterize members of an entire ethnic group. Misinformation about the perceived threat posed by the targeted group motivated violence against members of that group. In each instance, leaders convinced the public that failure to act out against the targeted group put their own lives and livelihoods in jeopardy. Failure to address the "Jewish Problem" would lead to the demise of Germans and Germany; failure to act against the Tutsis would allow them the opportunity to seize control and wield power over the Hutus; failure to act against the Rohingya would lead to the destruction of land, water, and people. We can see in each of these instances the role mass media, including newspapers, radio, and social media, played in the dissemination of these hateful messages. Media were the tools used to spread misinformation and convince members of the public to act, or at the very least, condone the violent actions of others. In every instance, media played an important role in disseminating and normalizing extremist viewpoints.

Impacts on Individuals

In addition to fueling bias-motivated violence and genocide on a societal level, hate speech also severely impacts individuals. A recent study published in *JAMA Pediatrics* found that public expressions of discrimination generate stress and behavioral health problems, particularly in racial/ethnic minority or socioeconomically disadvantaged youths.[19] In 2019, the American Academy of Pediatrics issued a report, which drew on 180 key studies, about the acute health dangers of racism on young people.

Laura Leets's 2002 study, "Experiencing Hate Speech: Perceptions and Responses to Anti-Semitism and Antigay Speech," exposed Jewish and LGBTQIA college students to harmful speech based on real scenarios. Leets found that the short- and long-term effects of participants' exposure to hate speech might be similar in form (but sometimes

Media were the tools used to spread misinformation and convince members of the public to act, or at the very least, condone the violent actions of others.

not in intensity) to the effects of other kinds of traumatic experiences.[20] Although the nature of emotional and psychological harm is hard to capture, short-term effects of victimization likely include feelings of shame, embarrassment, humiliation, anxiety, intimidation, anger, frustration, fear, or helplessness. Long-term impacts likely include continued anxiety and even depression.

In their seminal book on this topic, *Words That Wound: Critical Race Theory, Assaultive Speech, and the First Amendment,* scholars Mari J. Matsuda, Charles R. Lawrence III, Richard Delgado, and Kimberlé Williams Crenshaw characterize hate speech as assaultive speech that can have negative long-term effects on the individuals targeted.[21] Hate speech damages members of the defamed group by influencing them to believe in their own inferiority. Children are among the most vulnerable. When they are exposed to hate speech on a regular basis, they may eventually begin to question their own competence and self-worth.

Hate speech can also silence individuals and reduce their participation in the political process. Danielle Keats Citron and Helen Norton have argued that the cacophony of noise created by this vitriol actually works to limit civic engagement, particularly online. Citron and Norton developed a theory of digital citizenship, in which various online activities deepen civic engagement, political participation, and public conversation.[22] In her 2014 book on the subject, *Hate Crimes in Cyberspace,* Citron argues that cyber harassment and online hate speech enhances little of the process of political self-governance, working instead to destroy it.[23] Victims cannot participate in their online networks if they are under assault from a barrage of harmful slurs. Thus, the proliferation of hate speech makes it more difficult for women and people of color to engage in the political process, changing the nature of who is elected and which issues are considered most salient.

Why Do We Do It?

Given the negative short- and long-term consequences hate speech can have on individuals, why do we do it?

Social scientists have at least one explanation. Henri Tajfel's social identity theory suggests that the categorization of people into groups motivates us to seek positive social identity through comparisons between our group and other groups. As part of this comparative process, people degrade members of other groups as a way to maintain their own positive social identity. In other words, putting members of other groups down makes us feel more secure in our group membership and reinforces our identity. By using slurs to label a member of a different ethnic group, we reinforce our identity as a member of our own group. Moreover, this process also functions to maintain the existing social order. Hate speech is a way to remind members of other groups of your own group's position of dominance.

What Do We Do about It?

Now that we know what hate speech is and what it does, the question remains, what should be done about it?

For many nations, the solution to this problem is a legal one. As we'll see in the next chapter, many countries have taken steps to prohibit and criminally punish hate speech in an effort to minimize its role in inciting violence and creating the climate for discrimination. Sometimes, this takes the form of media regulation, as media platforms attempt to minimize the spread of this kind of expression.

People also react to hate speech through social stigmatization. Although permitted in public places in the United States, hate speech in the workplace has severe consequences, and the public generally reacts to the use of hate speech by celebrities or politicians by shunning them, at least for a little while. In 2018, comedian Roseanne Barr posted a racist tweet about a former member of the Obama administration, Valerie Jarrett, implying that she was the lovechild of the Muslim Brotherhood and Planet of the Apes. Barr's show on ABC, *Roseanne*, was immediately canceled by the network. Along those lines, comedian

Michael Richards, of Seinfeld fame, fell out of the public eye after using the N-word in his stand-up routine. Notably, however, the consequences for public figures are not always severe or lasting. In 2010, conservative radio host Laura Ingraham used the N-word several times on air and is now a host on the Fox News Channel, proving that the unapologetic use of hate speech does not always result in irreparable damage to one's career.

While each of these reactions seeks to minimize the spread and impact of hate speech, the phenomenon continues to exist, both in person and online. Moving forward, we need to consider how to best address this issue. While censorship of hate speech may feel like a viable option, there are valid concerns about the impact of censorship on freedom of expression. On the other hand, failure to address the proliferation of hate speech harms individuals' dignity and can have grave consequences at a societal level, including bias-motivated violence.

INTERNATIONAL APPROACHES
TO SOLVING THE PROBLEM
OF HATE SPEECH

No country or culture is immune to the problem of hate speech. International bodies such as the United Nations, the European Commission, and the European Union, as well as individual countries, have tried to legally prohibit or punish hate speech in different ways. This chapter examines how Germany, Canada, Brazil, South Africa, Japan, and the United States regulate hate speech (or don't), and the effects these efforts have on public discourse. Given that laws are not created in a vacuum but instead are shaped by social, economic, and political forces, the examination of each country's approach will consider how the unique history, culture, and people of each nation have influenced their views on hate speech. The themes that emerge from this analysis showcase how countries balance respect for religion, gender, and other protected categories of identity with citizens' rights to free expression, their right to dignity, and their right to religious freedom.

United Nations

After World War II ended, 50 governments drafted the charter of the United Nations to prevent future wars. Recognizing the atrocities of the Holocaust, the work of this intergovernmental organization began in part with the creation of the Universal Declaration of Human Rights (UDHR) in 1948, which established that all humans are equal and are deserving of equal protection under the law. The UDHR provides protection against discrimination or incitement, and establishes the right to freedom of expression, although not absolutely. A country may limit those rights provided that the law is precise and pursues a legitimate aim (such as the protection of national security or of public order, or of public health or morals). Nevertheless, the state must establish a direct and immediate connection between the expression and the threat in order to demonstrate the necessity of that limitation and the appropriate proportionality of the specific action.

The next major effort from the UN regarding free expression developed as a response to the civil rights movements across the globe during the 1960s. The UN adopted the International Covenant on Civil and Political Rights

(ICCPR), which says that "advocacy of national, racial, or religious hatred that constitutes incitement to discrimination, hostility, or violence shall be prohibited by law." However, states must show that the harm of discrimination cannot be lessened by means other than the suppression of speech, such as the use of educational initiatives. Around the same time, the UN also adopted the International Convention on the Elimination of All Forms of Racial Discrimination (ICERD), which requires signatories to condemn all propaganda and organizations based on ideas of racial or ethnic superiority, while still giving due regard to the right to freedom of thought, religion, opinion, expression, and peaceful assembly and association. Member states declared participation in organizations that promote racial discrimination (such as the Ku Klux Klan) punishable by law and prohibited public authorities or institutions from promoting or inciting racial discrimination. Notably, the ICERD and ICCPR seek to prevent or punish incitement to racial hatred rather than hate speech directly. According to Susan Benesch, a consultant to the UN Special Advisor on the Prevention of Genocide, incitement inspires an audience to harm a person or a group, while hate speech, which is not prohibited under ICERD or ICCPR conventions, is aimed directly at a victim. Instead, the ICERD and ICCPR are really about incitement to discrimination based on race, color, or ethnic origin.

In an effort to clarify what constitutes incitement to discrimination, the Office of the United Nations High Commissioner for Human Rights (OHCHR) organized a series of expert workshops in 2011. The resulting "Rabat Plan of Action" concluded that: "Prohibition should focus only on the advocacy of discriminatory hatred that constitutes incitement to hostility, discrimination, or violence, rather than the advocacy of hatred without regard to its tendency to incite action by the audience against a protected group."[1] In other words, incitement includes specific calls to violence or discrimination but not expression that simply advocates hatred. Under this framework, a White pride website would not be considered incitement unless it called on readers to deny jobs to people of color or commit violent crimes against them. In an effort to help states make judicial assessments about what constitutes incitement, the Rabat Plan included six specific factors of analysis:

1. The political, economic, and social context in which the expression was communicated. This includes a nation's history of institutionalized discrimination, the existing legal framework and media landscape.

2. The identity of the speaker. Incitement is more likely to occur when the speaker has authority over

their audience, such as a public official, politician, community or religious leader might.

3. The intent of the speaker to engage in advocacy to hatred against a protected group on the basis of a protected characteristic. If the speaker knows their speech is likely to incite discrimination, hostility, or violence, it is likely a violation of international law.

4. The content of the speech. The form and style of the expression, and whether it is understood by the audience, should be considered.

5. The magnitude or volume of the expression, as well as the means of expression should be considered. Advocacy to discrimination is likely to violate the law when it is disseminated widely via mass media.

6. The likelihood that harm will occur as a direct result of the incitement. The imminence of harm should be taken into account.[2]

Most recently, questions about the applicability of the ICCPR to online content have arisen. In 2012, the UN Human Rights Council recognized that the same rights people have offline must apply online. Limitations on electronic communications should therefore be justified in the same way that offline prohibitions are. However, the UN Special Rapporteur on the Promotion and Protection of the Right to Freedom of Opinion and Expression has made clear that private entities, such as social media platforms, should not be responsible for enacting censorship measures. Therefore, demands to remove content from these platforms must be based on states' existing laws.

In 2017, the UN Special Rapporteur on Freedom of Expression adopted a Joint Declaration on Freedom of Expression and "Fake News," Disinformation, and Propaganda.[3] The declaration strongly restates the position that intermediaries, like Web-hosting platforms or social media sites, should never be held liable for content posted by third parties unless they specifically intervene in that content or refuse a court order to remove it. The declaration also calls on intermediaries to be transparent in their removal process. Under these guidelines, Facebook or Google would not be held responsible for posts or websites created by users and uploaded to their platforms.

Incitement to Hatred Based on Religion, Gender, Gender Identity, and Sexual Orientation

The United Nations declarations and conventions discussed thus far have focused exclusively on preventing incitement to hatred based on race, ethnicity, or national origin. However, as Nazila Ghanea said in her paper presented to the UN Committee on the Elimination of Racial Discrimination, it may be time for a more intersectional approach to dealing with racist hate speech.[4] "Discrimination on the basis of race, color, descent, or national or ethnic origin exists," she said, "but it is overlaid or compounded by other discriminations as well, such as religion." The Organization of Islamic Cooperation (OIC) pushed for the *Combatting Defamations of Religions* resolution in 2009 in response to the Danish newspaper *Jyllands-Posten* mocking the Prophet Muhammad and the resulting riots. The United States and most other Western democracies rejected it, arguing that prohibiting speech is not the way to promote tolerance, because the "defamations of religions" concept is then used to justify censorship, criminalization, and in some cases, violent assaults and deaths of political, racial, and religious minorities around the world. The OIC eventually abandoned the resolution against religious defamation, instead partnering with Western nations to support a new resolution: *Combating Intolerance, Negative Stereotyping and Stigmatization of, and Discrimination, Incitement to Violence, and Violence against Persons Based on Religion or Belief.*

This resolution adopts a very Western, liberal position on freedom of expression, criminalizing incitement to violence based on religion or belief, but also protecting free expression and honoring respectful debate and interfaith dialogue as ways of combatting religious hatred and incitement. However, this resolution left the outcome unclear if religious expression is the root cause of hatred toward members of a protected class. For example, does the right to freedom of expression allow me to disparage Islam because it goes against my own religious beliefs? The European Court of Human Rights addressed this issue in 2018, asking whether an individual's right to free expression extended to include insults to the Prophet Muhammad. The European Court said that the right to free expression did not protect denigrating another's religion, upholding the conviction of an Austrian woman who was fined for comparing scripturally based behavior of the prophet to pedophilia.

In addition to confusion about how the right to freedom of expression interacts with the right to religious expression, the UN's framework also fails to provide an exhaustive list of protected classes or characteristics. Thus, each individual signatory must decide whether its laws will prohibit incitement to hatred based on sexual orientation and/or gender identity. For example, Japan does not recognize gender identity or sexual orientation as protected classes, while Ireland does.

Ultimately, the UN's framework fails to resolve the tension between balancing the right to free expression and the prohibitions against incitement to racial hatred. Article IV of the ICERD says that parties to the convention must also make it illegal to disseminate ideas based on racial superiority or hatred, or engage in incitement to racial hatred or incitement to acts of violence, while Article V of the same convention provides protection for freedom of expression. The due regard clause of Article IV calls on states to restrict expression only when other efforts, such as education, have failed. Thus, states have tended to give greater weight to freedom of expression when enacting legislation associated with Article IV. According to Amnesty International, robust protection of freedom of expression is a "powerful and essential tool for combating racial discrimination and violence."[5] The solution to the problem of racial, national, and ethnic hatred, says Amnesty International, is more, not less, speech. However, this approach means that oftentimes expression that leads to bias-motivated violence, like that described in the Anti-Defamation League's Pyramid of Hate in chapter 1, goes unchecked. At the end of the day, signatories to all of these conventions are free to determine which cases they prosecute, which means that all of these international protections lack teeth if violations of national criminal and civil laws aren't prosecuted.

Council of Europe

European countries banded together after World War II to create the Council of Europe, which today includes 47 countries. Member countries must maintain certain standards of human rights and democracy, including democratically elected parliaments, legal systems with democratic principles, and a system for protection of national minorities. However, the Council is primarily a treaty-making entity whose actions have no legal ramifications without signature and ratification by member countries. Like the United Nations, the European Council has its own Convention on Human Rights that both protects the right to free expression and information, and prevents discrimination on any grounds including sex, race, color, language, religion, political or other opinion, national or social origin, association with a national minority, property, birth, or other status.

In 1993, the Council of Europe established the European Commission Against Racism and Intolerance (ECRI) to tackle the problem of hate speech directly by issuing a *Plan of Action on Combating Racism, Xenophobia, Anti-Semitism, and Intolerance.* After first reviewing member states' existing legislation, the Commission raised several issues regarding the use of the internet to spread anti-Semitic propaganda and the lack of enforcement of internet regulations by member states. Responding to the findings of their investigation, the ECRI moved to include the suppression of hate speech in the pending *Convention on Cybercrime* to empower law enforcement to take more cooperative and efficient action against the dissemination of hate speech, along with copyright infringement, child pornography, and other issues. However, in 2003, when the United States clarified that it would not sign the *Convention on Cybercrime* if the issue of internet hate speech were included, the ECRI made the *Additional Protocol on Internet Hate Speech* a separate protocol in order to secure the United States' endorsement of the *Convention on Cybercrime*. The *Additional Protocol on Internet Hate Speech* calls for an update to countries' offline laws so that they also prohibit racist or xenophobic material online. The *Additional Protocol* defines this content as: "Any written material, any image or any other representation of ideas or theories, which advocates, promotes or incites hatred, discrimination or violence, against any individual or group of individuals, based on race, color, descent or national or ethnic origin, as well as religion if used as a pretext for any of these factors."[6] Specifically, the *Protocol* requires parties to criminalize five types of conduct:

1. Each party must criminalize distributing or otherwise making available racist and xenophobic material to the public through a computer system.

2. The *Additional Protocol* requires each country to criminalize the act of directing a threat to a person through the internet purely because of race, national origin or religion.

3. The *Protocol* requires each country to criminalize the act of publicly insulting a person through a computer system because of their race, national origin or religion.

4. Each party must pass legislation making it a crime to distribute or make available through the internet material which denies, grossly minimizes, approves or justifies acts constituting genocide or crimes against humanity.

5. The *Protocol* provides for extradition between parties.

While this multilateral effort may be commendable, the *Protocol* has its problems. The European Council has chosen to primarily relieve internet service providers (ISPs) of responsibility for hateful or incendiary material published on their sites. Instead, the *Protocol* makes individuals posting racist content liable and limits the liability of third-party intermediaries. Notably, the *Protocol* leaves room for countries to adopt an expansive definition of intent, meaning that third parties may be liable if they receive notification of racist or xenophobic expression on their platform and fail to remove it. For example, Germany's Information and Communications Service Act of 1997 holds ISPs liable if they know of the content, have the ability to block it, but fail to take remedial action. Finally, because the *Additional Protocol on Internet Hate Speech* focuses almost exclusively on criminal penalties, it fails to take into consideration the extent to which civil remedies might be used as an effective deterrent.

European Union

As a political and economic union dedicated to promoting peace and economic prosperity, the European Union (EU) is committed to fairness and respect for all cultures and languages. To that end, the Charter of Fundamental Rights of the European Union establishes human dignity as inviolable and deserving of protection and respect, providing the right to freedom of expression and opinion, along with the right to receive and impart information without interference of public authority. It provides equal protection under the law and the right to be free from discrimination based on sex, race, color, ethnic or social origin, genetic features, language, religion or belief, political or any other opinion, membership of a national minority, property, birth, disability, age, sexual orientation, or nationality. The Charter also dedicates portions to respecting cultural, religious, and linguistic diversity, as well as establishing equality between men and women.

To address the problem of hate speech specifically, in 2008, the EU adopted the *Framework Decision on Combating Certain Forms and Expressions of Racism and Xenophobia by Means of Criminal Law*. This law requires states to sanction racism and xenophobia through "effective, proportionate and dissuasive criminal penalties." The EU calls out specific conduct as hate speech, including:

- public incitement to violence or hatred directed against a group of persons or a member of such a group defined on the basis of race, color, descent, religion or belief, or national or ethnic origin;

- the above-mentioned offense when carried out by the public dissemination or distribution of tracts, pictures, or other material;

- publicly condoning, denying, or grossly trivializing crimes of genocide, crimes against humanity, and war crimes when the conduct is carried out in a manner likely to incite violence or hatred against such a group or a member of such a group;

- instigating, aiding, or abetting in the commission of the above offenses is also punishable.

Each of these actions is punishable by effective, proportionate, and dissuasive penalties and a term of imprisonment up to a maximum of at least one year.

The EU's E-Commerce Directive provides the legal framework for ISPs' and other third-party intermediaries' responsibilities regarding hate speech on their online platforms. Under this directive, ISPs do not have a duty to monitor conduct and are governed by the laws of the member state in which they are established. Jurisdictional issues continue to prove problematic, particularly in instances where content is created in countries that allow hate speech but accessed in those that prohibit it. In *Yahoo!, Inc. v. La Ligue Contre Le Racisme et L'antisemitisme* (LICRA), two French student organizations instituted action against Yahoo! for selling Nazi merchandise on its auction website, which was prohibited by French law. A French court ordered Yahoo! to remove the content within three months or be fined a penalty of 100,000 francs per day. Yahoo! appealed the action in the United States, and eventually the Ninth Circuit found that there was no basis for jurisdiction because LICRA and UEJF had insufficient contacts with the forum's home country. Neither the US District Court nor the US Court of Appeals answered the question about the chilling effect enforcement would have, and thus it remains unclear as to whether the lack of jurisdiction acts as a barrier to enforcement.

In addition to international bodies such as the United Nations and the European Union, individual countries are also working to address the issue of hate speech. For some countries, such as Germany, this means crafting strict legal prohibitions against the creation and dissemination of hate speech, both in person and online. For others, such as the United States, this involves carving out narrow categories of exception, such as true threats or incitement, to the near absolute protection of hate speech afforded under the First Amendment. For all of these countries, the process of regulating hate speech is complex and nuanced as each seeks to balance citizens' right to dignity with their right to freedom of expression.

Germany

Given its history, Germany's stringent laws restricting hate speech come as no surprise. At the international level, Germany is a member state of the European Commission on Human Rights and a signatory of major United Nations initiatives, such as the ICCPR and the ICERD. The 1949 German Constitution, or "Grundgesetz," begins by establishing that human dignity is inviolable. The right to dignity trumps most other rights, such as the right to free expression and press. The constitution specifically states that a person who abuses free expression in order to combat the free democratic order shall forfeit basic rights. Thus, the right to free expression in Germany is not absolute, but can be limited when it offends the constitutional order or moral code.

Germany's Criminal Code includes provisions for bias-motivated crimes as well as "symbolic" crimes. Like hate crime statutes in the United States, German courts will take an offender's racist or xenophobic motives into account during the sentencing of any crime. Most hate speech, though, falls under the category of symbolic

The process of regulating hate speech is complex and nuanced as each country seeks to balance citizens' right to dignity with their right to freedom of expression.

crimes, and provides penalties for incitement to hatred, attacks on dignity, distribution of hate propaganda, and Holocaust denial. The first portion of the code states:

> Whoever, in a manner capable of disturbing the public peace 1). Incites hatred against a national, racial, religious group or a group defined by their ethnic origins, against segments of the population or individuals because of their belonging to one of the aforementioned groups or segments of the population or calls for violent or arbitrary measures against them; or 2). Assaults the human dignity of others by insulting, maliciously maligning an aforementioned group, segments of the population or individuals because of their belonging to one of the aforementioned groups or segments of the population, or defaming segments of the population, shall be liable to imprisonment from three months to five years.[7]

The second section addresses the distribution of hate propaganda, stating that those who disseminate materials that incite hatred or assault dignity, either in writing or via public displays, radio, media, or telecommunication services, or makes these materials accessible to a person under 18, can go to prison for up to three years or be subject to a fine.

Although Germany's Criminal Code did not originally include Holocaust denial as a specific prohibition, it was amended in the mid-1990s after a controversial ruling in the *Irving* case, which held that under the current law a pseudo-scientific explanation denying the Holocaust did not constitute an assault on dignity since there was no specific person injured by the comment. Today, the law prohibits publically approving of, denying, or downplaying acts committed under the rule of National Socialism. Individuals or groups who disturb the peace in a manner that violates the dignity of victims by approving of, glorifying, or justifying National Socialism may be punished under this law. While there is no specific test used by judges to interpret or apply these sanctions, courts (specifically in the 1994 *Irving* case) have generally considered the intent of the expression and its truthfulness. Courts will also look at the manner of distribution of hate propaganda, the size of the audience receiving the information, and whether the issue is a matter of public concern.

In addition to prohibiting expression that incites hatred and assaults human dignity, the German Criminal Code also criminalizes two forms of group defamation. First, the Criminal Code outlaws collective defamation, which involves statements made about entire groups, such as the Central Council of Jews in Germany. Secondly, the code criminalizes defamation about groups, which includes defamatory statements targeting members of a group that can be identified by their protected characteristics. However, in the past, German courts dismissed cases brought by Jewish people against anti-Semites, arguing these cases actionable only when they are directed at specific groups. For example, comments about the "Prussian judges" could be the basis for a suit, whereas comments about Jewish people could not.

In addition to criminal libel, Germany also provides several pathways for victims of hate speech to pursue civil claims. Citizens may pursue monetary damages caused by the commission of a crime such as incitement to hatred, insult, and defamation. Those targeted by hate speech can also pursue civil claims for the torts associated with "protection of personality rights" and "immoral intentional damages." Finally, victims of hate speech may also file claims under the anti-discrimination provisions of the 2006 General Act on Equal Treatment (AGG). The AGG prohibits both direct and indirect discrimination, harassment, and sexual harassment based on race or ethnic origin, gender, sexual orientation, religion, disability, or age.

German law also prohibits hate speech in broadcast communications. Some German regulations apply to content generally, while other regulations specifically aim to protect children. The Youth Protection Act empowers the Office for the Examination of Materials Endangering Youths to maintain a list of materials that endangers the well-being of young people, including several well-known

American video games such as *Wolfenstein 3D*, *Resident Evil*, *Medal of Honor*, *Mortal Kombat*, and *Quake*. This office has also banned the sale of neo-Nazi music to young people.

Germany is also an international leader in shaping standards for online communication and content. In 1997, Germany passed the Multimedia Law, which aims to keep illegal material out of cyberspace and update the previously written statutes to address the technology of the twenty-first century.

Canada

Like Germany, some countries outside the European Union also maintain strict hate speech laws. Canada sees itself as a multi-ethnic/racial country that seeks to protect the rights of all people regardless of their gender, gender identity, race, age, or sexual orientation. The Canadian Charter of Rights and Freedoms establishes citizens' fundamental freedoms, including their right to freedom of thought, belief, opinion, and expression, as well as freedom of the press and other media. It also provides for equal rights among citizens, and it holds that everyone has the right to equal protection and benefit of the law without discrimination based on race, national or ethnic origin, color, religion, sex, age, or mental or physical disability, which essentially establishes affirmative action as constitutional. However, these rights are not absolute. The first section of the Charter specifically states that the rights and freedoms outlined therein may be subject to "reasonable limits prescribed by law as can be demonstrably justified in a free and democratic society."

Among those reasonable limitations are criminal laws prohibiting hate speech. The Canadian Criminal Code includes federal and provincial laws that levy fines or prison time against: "Everyone who, by communicating statements, other than in private conversation, willfully promotes hatred against any identifiable group is guilty of (a) an indictable offense and is liable to imprisonment for a term not exceeding two years; or (b) an offense punishable on summary conviction" (Section 319(2)). The law goes on to clarify that:

> No person shall be convicted under subsection (2) (a) if he establishes that the statements communicated were true; (b) if, in good faith, the person expressed or attempted to establish by an argument an opinion on a religious subject or an opinion based on a belief in a religious text; (c) if the statements were relevant to any subject of public interest, the discussion of which was for the public benefit, and if on reasonable grounds he believed them to be true; or (d) if, in good faith, he intended

to point out, for the purpose of removal, matters producing or tending to produce feelings of hatred toward an identifiable group in Canada.

The Criminal Code also prohibits advocacy of genocide and incitement to violence, and provides for the seizure of hate propaganda that is published or the erasure of hate propaganda from a computer system. In 2004, Canada updated the law to designate sexual orientation as a protected category.

Other Canadian laws include provisions that limit the spread and impact of hate speech. The Canada Post Corporation Act allows for the denial of mail privileges if hate propaganda is being transmitted. The Customs Tariff Act prohibits hate propaganda from being imported into Canada. The Broadcasting Distribution Regulations prohibit the broadcasting of "any abusive comment or abusive pictorial representation that, when taken in context, tends to or is likely to expose an individual or group or class of individuals to hatred or contempt on the basis of race, national origin, color, religion, sex, sexual orientation, age, or mental or physical disability." In 2019, Prime Minister Justin Trudeau enacted a digital charter to police and punish social media and online sites that promote hate.

The constitutionality of the laws outlined here has held up through multiple judicial challenges. In *Regina v. Andrews* (1990), the leader of a White supremacist nationalist party and distributor of the bimonthly magazine *National Reporter*, was charged under Section 319(2) of the Canadian Criminal Code for willfully promoting hatred against an identifiable group. The Supreme Court found that Andrews's arrest did violate Section 2 of the Charter, which provides the right to free expression. However, the arrest was valid under Section 1 of the Charter, which states that the rights outlined in the Charter are subject to reasonable limits.

In *Regina v. Keegstra* (1990), the Canadian Supreme Court upheld a criminal conviction of a high school teacher who communicated anti-Semitic propaganda to his pupils. The teacher said in class that Jewish people were "treacherous," "subversive," "sadistic," "money-loving," "power-hungry," and "child killers." The court ruled that hate propaganda like this does not warrant protection because it undermines respect among diverse racial, religious, and cultural groups rather than promoting any genuine expression of value. Notably, the court in *Keegstra* considered the impact on the targeted group (Jewish Canadians) as well as the non-targeted group (all Canadians). The court argued that the teacher's expression should be punished because not only would it degrade, humiliate, and diminish the self-worth of Jewish Canadians, but it may also cause *all* Canadians to become more accepting of messages of racial or religious inferiority. In addition to being concerned with prohibiting speech that incites immediate violent action against members of a particular group, the Canadian judiciary recognized the long-term harm to social cohesion that could be caused by unchecked hate speech.

To be prosecuted under the Canadian Criminal Code, the accused must have intentionally committed the relevant act with awareness of the nature of their actions. However, there are also noncriminal sanctions found in the Canadian Human Rights Act (CHRA) that do not require that the accused had intended their expression to discriminate. This legislation does not focus on punishment or deterrence, but instead on promoting equality and anti-discrimination. For example, Section 12 of the CHRA establishes that it is discriminatory to publicly publish or display "any notice, sign, symbol, emblem, or other representation that (a) expresses or implies discrimination or an intention to discriminate, or (b) incites or is calculated to incite others to discriminate." Furthermore:

> It is a discriminatory practice for a person or a group of persons acting in concert to communicate telephonically or to cause to be so communicated, repeatedly in whole or in part by means of the facilities of a telecommunication undertaking within the legislative authority of Parliament, any matter that is likely to expose a person or persons to hatred or contempt by reason of the fact that that person or those persons are identifiable on the basis of a prohibited ground of discrimination.

The case *Canada Human Rights Commission v. Taylor* (1990) upheld the constitutionality of this law. The majority of the court found that the law justifiably limits freedom of expression, arguing that "hate propaganda produces effects that are deleterious to the objective of equality of opportunity. Thus, there is clearly a rational connection between the restriction on communicating hate messages and the objective of promoting equality for racial and religious minorities."

Despite this ruling, courts have not consistently found all hateful messages to be a violation of the federal Human Rights Act or similar regional provisions. In 2006, the case *Owens v. Saskatchewan Human Rights Commission* challenged Saskatchewan's Human Rights Code. Hugh Owens placed an ad in the *Saskatoon Star Phoenix* featuring two stick figures holding hands with a circle around them and a line through it, along with references to Bible verses from Leviticus stating that "if a *man* also lie with mankind as he lieth with a woman, both of them have committed an abomination. They *shall* surely be *put to death*."

The court declared that the ad, one of many that Owens placed in various papers throughout the 2000s, did not violate Saskatchewan's Human Rights Code because Canadians have a constitutional right to express their sincere religious opinions publicly. The Criminal Code contains a religious exception, stating that a person may not be convicted for expressing an argument or opinion on a

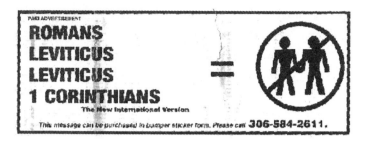

Figure 3 This ad, placed by Hugh Owens in the *Saskatoon Star Phoenix*, is considered protected expression under the religious exception to Canada's Criminal Code banning hate speech.

religious subject or an opinion based on a belief in a religious text.

Even with this provision, the Canadian Human Rights Act continued to face challenges. Tensions erupted when *Maclean's*, a Canadian current affairs and news magazine, published cartoons featuring the Prophet Muhammad. The magazine then refused to publish a critique written by law students contradicting some of the offensive conclusions implied by the cartoons and accompanying articles. In 2008, Professor Richard Moon was asked to formally examine Section 13(1) of the CHRA, which allowed federal and provincial Human Rights Commissions to investigate incidences of hate speech. His analysis concluded with the recommendation that the law be repealed and that only threats of violence be designated as punishable. In 2013, the Canadian Parliament acted on this recommendation and repealed the law.

This repeal happened despite the Supreme Court of Canada's reaffirmation of the constitutionality of provisions like Section 13(1) in the case *Saskatchewan Human Rights Commission v. Whatcott* (2013). Here, the Supreme Court found that the removal of fliers created by William Whatcott, which promoted hatred against individuals for their sexual orientation (one was titled "Keep Homosexuality out of Saskatoon's Public Schools!" and "Sodomites in Our Public Schools"), was a justified limitation on free expression.

In the *Whatcott* case, the Canadian Supreme Court once again affirmed its decision to censor hate speech based not only on its immediate impacts, but also on its long-term harm to society and potential to cause discrimination, segregation, violence, and even genocide. The court wrote:

> Hate speech is an effort to marginalize individuals based on their membership in a group. Using expression that exposes the group to hatred, hate speech seeks to delegitimize group members in the eyes of the majority, reducing their social standing and acceptance within society. Hate speech, therefore, rises beyond causing distress to individual group members. It can have a societal

impact. Hate speech lays the groundwork for later, broad attacks on vulnerable groups that can range from discrimination, to ostracism, segregation, deportation, violence and, in the most extreme cases, to genocide. Hate speech also impacts on a protected group's ability to respond to the substantive ideas under debate, thereby placing a serious barrier to their full participation in our democracy.[8]

Clearly, tensions remain high in Canada between groups and individuals who seek to protect free expression and those who feel that the short- and long-term impacts of hate speech on the public sphere warrant its prohibition. Despite the removal of Section 13(1), the Canadian Criminal Code still prohibits most hate speech. However, without the support of federal and provincial human rights commissions, the investigation of these incidents will be left to police.

Brazil

Like many countries, including Germany, South Africa, and the United States, Brazil has struggled with racism and discrimination for decades. The country has a history of slavery, large immigrant communities, and a majority Christian population that is in tension with the

"Hate speech lays the groundwork for later, broad attacks on vulnerable groups that can range from discrimination, to ostracism, violence and, in the most extreme cases, to genocide."

Afro-Brazilian religions practiced by many of its citizens. Afro-Brazilians make up 49.4 percent of the population, feeding into the myth that the country is racially harmonious, when in fact there is substantial financial and social inequality between members of various groups. Wage inequities of up to 40 percent exist between Whites and Afro-Brazilians with the same level of education.[9]

In the 1950s, Brazil attempted to address this racial inequality after a famous African American ballerina was denied service at a prominent hotel in Rio de Janeiro. In response to that incident, the Brazilian Congress approved a law making practices resulting from racial prejudice a "contravention" or misdemeanor. However, during the 37 years the law was in effect, no one was convicted. In 1988, Brazil adopted the Citizens' Constitution as it re-democratized after a long period of dictatorship. The constitution set forth laws to protect human dignity and to "promote the well-being of all, without prejudice as to origin, race, sex, color, age, and any other forms of discrimination." The Citizens' Constitution also included protections for the right to freedom of expression. However, this freedom was not absolute and could not be used to infringe on the dignity of another. Brazil also adopted the Cao Act, named after its author, which affirmed that crimes resulting from discrimination based on race, color, ethnicity, religion, or national origin would be punished. Among other things, this law criminalized business owners who denied access to their establishments and ensured all students could attend school. However, this law focused primarily on physical access to places, rather than symbolic discrimination.

To address that issue, Brazil amended the law against racism in 1997 to prohibit "practicing, inducing, or inciting discrimination or prejudice of race, color, ethnicity, religion, or national origin," which is now punishable by one to three years in jail and a fine. This law also makes it illegal to manufacture, commercialize, distribute, or transport symbols, emblems, ornaments, badges, or advertisements that use the swastika for purposes of spreading Nazism in Brazil, or to commit these crimes through the media or publication of any nature. Brazil had been a stronghold of the Nazi Party in the years before World War II, and many Nazi war criminals, including Josef Mengele, fled to Brazil to hide among the German-Brazilian communities after the war ended. In 2003, Brazilian writer Siegfried Ellwanger was sentenced to two years imprisonment for his anti-Semitic books such as *Holocaust: Jewish or German? The Creators of the Lie of the Century, Hitler: Guilty or Innocent,* and *The Conquerors of the World: The True Criminals of War*.[10]

The law against racism also provided the language for a new category of an aggravated form of libel known as "racial disparagement." This provision states that libel claims may be brought when an individual's dignity or decorum has been offended based on the use of elements referring to race, color, ethnicity, religion, origin, or personal condition of old age or disability. Notably, gender, gender identity, or sexual orientation are not included in this list, and thus cannot be grounds for lawsuits at this time.

Before Brazil amended this law in 2009, racism and racial disparagement were the only two options for classifying disputes. Racism was considered a crime and the appropriate prosecutor's office filed charges. Private attorneys filed racial disparagement claims in cases where criminal liability could be removed through civil agreement on recovery of damages or a plea bargain. After 2009, victims could file public criminal complaints at the prosecutor's office.[11]

Despite having several applicable criminal and civil laws on the books, there are still very few convictions in Brazil for hate speech, particularly hate speech directed at Afro-Brazilians. In 1996, a civil public action case focused on a song by Francisco Everado Oliveira Silva called "Look at Her Hair" (*Veja os cabelos dela*) about the "inherent distasteful animal smell of black women and the ugliness of their natural hair."[12]

The lyrics said:

When she passes she calls my attention, but her hair, there's no way no. Her catinga [African] (body odor) almost caused me to faint. Look, I cannot stand her odor. Look, look, look at her hair! It looks like a scouring pad for cleaning pans. I already told her to wash herself. But she insisted and didn't want to listen to me. This smelly *negra* . . . Stinking animal that smells worse than a skunk.

The judge found no criminal intent to offend Black women and the plaintiffs lost the criminal case. However, the plaintiffs won the civil suit on the grounds that authorship of the lyrics was discriminatory and insulting, and injurious to Black youth (the singer often appeared in a clown costume). Silva was ordered to pay 300,000 real ($162,000) in damages plus attorneys' fees.

Tanya Kateri Hernandez, a professor at Fordham Law School and author of the book *Racial Subordination in Latin America*,[13] argues that even successful criminal prosecutions are problematic because they treat racism as the work of isolated individuals, ignoring the structural or institutional nature of racism. Brazil portrays racists as criminals rather than representatives of long-standing racist cultural values. Hernandez calls for clearer civil actions with higher standards of evidence, rather than criminal punishments.

Today, though, victims use both civil and criminal laws against hate speech and racism to punish perpetrators and recoup damages for disparaging remarks made either in person or online. In 2005, Brazilian authorities detained an Argentine soccer player for racist shouts during a game and prosecuted a columnist in the Amazon for writing that government officials "could not stand the odor exhaled by Indians." In 2010, the Pernambuco Bar Association filed a request to open a criminal case against law student Mayara Petruso for racist comments made on Twitter about Northeasterners, who are predominantly Afro-Brazilians. On Twitter, Petruso said: "Northeastern is not us. Do a favor to SP [Sao Paulo]: kill a northeasterner, drowned." Later, she wrote on Facebook that allowing people in the Northeast to vote threatened to "sink the country who worked to support the bums." The court sentenced Petruso to one year, five months, and fifteen days in prison, which was eventually converted into community service and a fine.

Despite the handful of prosecutions and even convictions that have occurred, hate speech is extremely prevalent in Brazil's public discourse, in part because of Brazilian President Jair Bolsonaro, who many worry has institutionalized hate speech despite existing laws against it. Elected in 2018, Bolsonaro has regularly advocated violence against members of the LGBTQIA community, saying gay children should be whipped in order to be reformed, and calling for the murder of organizers of pro-LGBTQIA events. He called a congresswoman a slut and referred to a woman journalist as an "uneducated idiot." He also targets non-White people outside of Brazil, describing immigrants from Haiti, Senegal, Bolivia, and Syria as "the scum of the world."

President Bolsonaro's actions are at odds with the country's purported stance against prejudiced comments. His continued, unchecked use of hate speech serves as an example of how unevenly and at times unfairly these rules can be applied. In Brazil, prosecution of hate speech depends largely on who is speaking, who is targeted, and how public the incidences are. In the case of Bolsonaro, a commitment to fight violent crime in the country has given him a pass to disparage individuals based on their gender, sexual orientation, and/or race.

South Africa

While extremism is gaining a new foothold in Brazil, South Africa has long suffered the consequences of dictatorship. While the rules may have said one thing, the reality was often quite different. Before apartheid ended, the South African government had already outlawed speech advocating national or racial hatred. Although the prohibition was supposed to be race neutral, it was often used to silence anti-apartheid expression. The use of hate speech prohibitions to silence anti-White sentiments persists today and problematizes the country's current approach to restricting and punishing hate speech. However, the new Bill of Rights established as part of the new constitution included a framework for prohibiting hate speech and contained protections for freedom of expression that include press freedom, the right to information, freedom of artistic creativity, and academic freedom. Section two of that provision says that the right to free expression does not extend to war propaganda, incitement to imminent violence, or "advocacy of hatred that is based on race, ethnicity, gender, or religion, and that constitutes incitement to cause harm." This provision does not automatically designate "advocacy of hatred" as a criminal or civil offense, but provides a category of speech that is not subject to constitutional protection and can be regulated by the state. The new Bill of Rights also established the right to equal protection under the law and the right to dignity, stating that the rights provided in the constitution may be limited by a law of general application only "to the extent that the limitation is reasonable and justifiable in an open and democratic society based on human dignity, equality, and freedom."

The constitutionality of these provisions in the Bill of Rights has rarely been challenged. In a fairly straightforward case, the South African Jewish Board of Deputies brought a complaint to the state-run Independent Broadcasting Agency for a violation of the Code of Conduct for Broadcasting Services. This clause prohibited broadcasting material that "is indecent or obscene or offensive to public morals or offensive to the religious convictions or feelings of any section of the population or likely to prejudice relations between sections of the population." The Islamic Unity Convention aired a program called "Zionism and Israel: An in-depth analysis." In the program, one of the interviewees "questioned the legitimacy of the State of Israel and Zionism as a political ideology, asserted that Jewish people were not gassed in concentration camps during the Second World War but died of infectious diseases, particularly typhus, and that only a million Jews had died." The Constitutional Court invalidated the Broadcasting Code, finding it overbroad and vague.

In 2006, the High Court in Johannesburg honored an Islamic organization's petition to prevent media conglomerates from publishing disparaging cartoons or caricatures of the prophet Muhammad. After controversy and violence erupted worldwide when a Danish paper published such cartoons, the High Court said free expression must be construed in the context of other values such as freedom, equality, and dignity.[14]

In 2010, South Africa enacted the Promotion of Equality and Prevention of Unfair Discrimination Act (PEPUDA), which prohibited unfair discrimination by the government and by private organizations or individuals, forbidding hate speech and harassment. The act specifically prohibited discrimination based on race, gender, sex, pregnancy, family responsibility or status, marital status, ethnic or social origin, HIV/AIDS status, color, sexual orientation, age, disability, religion, conscience, belief, culture, language, and birth. The act established divisions of the High Court and Magistrates Courts as "Equality Courts," where individuals can bring civil cases. Criminal prosecutions of hate speech are also permitted in South Africa under a common law offense known as "crimen injuria," when someone "unlawfully and intentionally impairs the dignity or privacy of another person." In 2017, the Equality Court received 328 hate speech complaints, up 36 percent from a year earlier, according to the Department of Justice. Of those, 125 were related to race.

Given the country's history with apartheid, the application of these extensive prohibitions remains complicated. For example, in 2011, Julius Malema, leader of the African National Congress Youth League, was found to have violated Section 10 of the Equality Act, which prohibits the publication of words involving the statute's protected classes that cause or perpetuate systemic disadvantage, undermine human dignity, or adversely affect the equal enjoyment of a person's rights and freedoms in a serious manner. Malema violated the act for singing lyrics denigrating Afrikaners, the White minority group that ruled South Africa during apartheid. The lyrics said, "Shoot the Bowe/farmer, shoot the Boers/farmers they are rapists/robbers."[15]

In a somewhat similar incident, a White South African named Penny Sparrow referred to Black South Africans as monkeys on her Facebook page. Velaphi Khumalo, a member of the ruling African National Congress, who is Black, responded to Sparrow's post on Facebook, saying that "white people in South Africa deserve to be hacked and killed like Jews." Sparrow was convicted and ordered to pay a fine, while the Equality Court ordered Khamalo to issue an apology to all South Africans.

In addition to the tension between Black and White South Africans, several public incidents of hate speech have also been directed at members of the LGBTQIA community. In 2008, the *Sunday Sun* ran an article by Dubula Jonathan Qwelane that compared gay and lesbian relationships to bestiality. The Equality Court found Qwelane guilty of violating the Equality Act, which prohibits propagation of hate toward members of the LGBTQIA community. Qwelane challenged Section 10 of the Equality Act as being vague, but the courts determined the law to be constitutional.

In an effort to create even stronger prohibitions against hate speech in the country, in 2018, South Africa passed the "Prevention and Combating of Hate Crimes and Hate Speech Bill." This new bill provides three- to five-year sentences for offenders who repeatedly publish, advocate, or communicate any intention to incite harm or propagate hatred based on one or more of the following grounds: age, albinism, birth, color, culture, disability, ethnic or social origin, gender or gender identity, HIV status, language, nationality, migrant or refugee status, race, religion, sex, or sexual orientation. Some South Africans view this law as progressive in its scope, while others say it goes too far in the limitations it places on expression, fearing that the rule may be used to silence political dissent.

Japan

Unlike South Africa, Japan is just now beginning to regulate hate speech, which has increased tremendously in the last few decades. Demonstrations by hate groups such as the Zaitokukai have recently brought the issue to the forefront of Japanese politics. The country's collective nature, its relatively homogenous population, and the peaceful coexistence of Shinto, Buddhist, and Christian populations are responsible, at least in part, for the relative lack of tension to date. That does not mean discrimination against indigenous populations such as the Burakumin and Ainu or against women and LGBTQIA folks has not existed, but those issues were not the subject of national debate. However, a low birthrate and labor shortage has increased immigration, changing the ethnic makeup of the country. Hate groups like the Zaitokukai have targeted foreigners, especially Korean and Chinese special permanent residents. Many of these individuals are refugees from World War II and the Korean War, or their descendants. They were born and raised in Japan but have been stripped of their citizenship. Reacting to the perceived privileges of ethnic Korean residents in particular, some Japanese have begun to publically display their animosity in rallies and demonstrations. At one now infamous rally, a young girl was caught on video screaming that Koreans should be massacred.

In 2007, the hate group Zaitokukai began participating in hundreds of demonstrations in Kyoto, Tokyo, Kawasaki City, and Osaka, home to a large population of ethnic Koreans. According to a 2015 study conducted by the Japanese government, Zaitokukai held 347 protests in 2013 and a total of over 1,200 between 2012 and 2015. As of 2017, the Zaitokukai boasted over sixteen thousand registered members.

A private Korean school in Kyoto brought forward the first legal case regarding direct harm caused by hate speech. The Kyoto Chosen Daiichi Primary School, which is operated by an educational corporation affiliated with the North Korean government, filed suit against the Zaitokukai for demonstrations at the school that referred to teachers, students, and staff as "cockroaches and maggots," and said that Koreans should be executed like dogs at public health centers. Zaitokukai members also publically claimed that "promises can be made between human beings but not humans and Koreans," and called on students to go back to the Korean Peninsula. In response to this dehumanizing language, the school brought both criminal

Figure 4 Members of the Zaitokukai protesting in 2013.
Source: CC BY-SA 2.0.

and civil charges against the Zaitokukai under existing
laws. They sought monetary damages and an injunction on
the group's behavior for Forcible Obstruction of Business,
Property Damages, and Defamation and Insult in the civil
code. Both the criminal and civil proceedings ended up at
the Supreme Court, where the Zaitokukai lost the cases.
They paid ¥12.2 million in damages, and were ordered not
to interact with teachers, students, or staff at the school.
The group was also prohibited from distributing leaflets,
picketing, or loitering within 200 meters of the school.

Interestingly, in the civil case, the court relied on the definition of discrimination provided by the ICERD, which requires parties to the convention to make it illegal to disseminate ideas based on racial superiority or hatred, or engage in incitement to racial hatred or incitement to acts of violence. However, the Japanese criminal and civil codes applicable in these cases apply only to statements about specific individuals and institutions, and thus are not the basis for prosecuting expression intended to foster hatred about an entire group. The Kyoto District Court said in its judgment that there could only be liability when the hateful speech was directed towards specific persons or associations.[16]

In response to this case and the growing visibility of the Zaitokukai demonstrations, the City of Osaka enacted its own ordinance against hate speech in January 2016. This ordinance recognized "the fact that hate speech may harm the dignity of an individual and cause a sense of discrimination towards them." In an attempt to curb hate speech and protect the human rights of the citizens, the Osaka ordinance defined hate speech as expression with the purpose of excluding or limiting the rights and freedoms of "any person or group of persons who has or have specific characteristics pertaining to race or ethnic origins from society."[17] If expression is deemed hate speech, the mayor is authorized to take measures necessary to prevent dissemination of any content and to announce the fact that the act constitutes hate speech along with the name of the actor. The Osaka ordinance also established the Osaka Hate Speech Review Board, a five-member group of academics and other experts selected to assist the mayor with investigations and deliberation on these matters.

Shortly after Osaka enacted this ordinance, Japan's legislature passed a federal law addressing the problem of hate speech. The Hate Speech Elimination Act does not criminalize discriminatory speech or behavior; instead, it deems an expression inappropriate and impermissible. Like many Japanese laws, this law relies on informal, positive social norms to mobilize compliance. The law itself contains seven articles. The first article establishes hate speech and declares that unjust and discriminatory words and deeds are not acceptable or appropriate. The second article defines unjust and discriminatory actions as those that incite exclusion of people from a country or region outside of Japan.

The term "unjust discriminatory words and deeds against people from outside Japan," as used in this act, means unjust words and deeds used to incite exclusion of people who are from a country or a region outside Japan or their descendants who live in Japan legally (hereinafter referred to as People from Outside Japan) from their local community because of their origin by intimidating them in public through a threat to their life, body, liberty, reputation, or property, or by severely insulting them, with the main purpose of boosting or inducing a sense of discrimination against them.

The law does not include minority groups from inside the country, such as members of the LGBTQIA community. Instead, this legislation only addresses harm done to foreigners, rather than marginalized groups of Japanese citizens. The third article of the Hate Speech Elimination Act declares the public responsible for furthering their own understanding of unfair discrimination, calling on them to engage in speech and behavior that eliminates it. Finally, Articles IV to VII of the act outline the responsibilities of local governments to support this effort. While there are not specific punishments laid out in the law, this rule will likely deny permits to groups such as the Zaitokukai for protest or use of government buildings for assembly. All protesters in Japan must obtain a permit from the local public safety commission before carrying out protests in public streets and parks. The City of Kawasaki cited the act in its decision to deny a permit to a racist group who wanted to protest in a diverse community.[18]

Legal scholar Craig Martin expressed concern that the new law's lack of meaningful sanctions or remedies may contribute to the continued, systematic violation of minority rights.[19] While the new law starts to acknowledge the plight of indigenous Japanese such as the Burakumin and Ainu, as well as the rights of women, foreigners, gays and lesbians, and minority groups such as Koreans and Chinese, Martin contends that it still leaves many members of these groups exposed to continued discrimination. In fact, the UN Human Rights Commission has reprimanded Japan for its failure to respect or enforce the ICERD's provision that member states must make it illegal to disseminate ideas based on racial superiority or hatred, or engage in incitement to racial hatred or acts of violence. Notably, the legislature had the option to include race and/or ethnicity in the Hate Speech Elimination Act, but chose not to.

Recognizing at least some of the issues with the 2016 law, including its lack of provisions to ban or punish discriminatory language against ethnic minorities, the Kawasaki Municipal Assembly recently passed a criminal ordinance against hate speech. Repeat violations involving language and actions against foreign people in public spaces in the city of Kawasaki will now be punishable by a fine of up to ¥500,000.

Moving forward, it will be interesting to see whether other municipalities pass their own criminal ordinances and whether or not that prompts the national legislature to revise its existing law. As of now, Japan has only begun to address the issue of hate speech in the country and thus has a long way to go toward developing comprehensive regulations that seek to protect the dignity of all of its citizens.

United States

While Japan is working to adopt laws discouraging the use of hate speech, in the United States, the First Amendment permits the use of hate speech in public and private discourse. Although hate speech is allowed under the law, the Civil Rights Act of 1964 prohibits discrimination related to employment or housing. Many states have also established hate crime legislation, which tacks on additional penalties for crimes motivated by the victim's race, ethnicity, sexual orientation, gender identity, etc. However, the First Amendment protects freedom of expression including hate speech in the United States. Unless hate speech falls into one of the categories of exception carved out by the Supreme Court, which include fighting words, incitement to violence, or true threats, it is protected by the First Amendment. In the past, individuals have also brought civil action under the torts of defamation and intentional infliction of emotional distress. However, the Supreme Court has generally rejected these cases. The categories of fighting words, incitement, and true threats will be examined in detail to demonstrate where the line between protected hate speech and prohibited expression exists.

The Supreme Court defined "fighting words" in the 1942 case *Chaplinsky v. New Hampshire*: "those personally abusive epithets which, when addressed to the ordinary citizen, are, as a matter of common knowledge, inherently likely to provoke a violent reaction." However, since the *Chaplinsky* decision, the Supreme Court has been reluctant to find much expression that falls within the narrow definition of this standard. For example, in *Terminiello v. Chicago*, the Supreme Court invalidated a breach of peace conviction against a man who denounced Jewish people to a crowd outside an auditorium as "slimy scum" and "bedbugs." The trial judge in that case instructed the jury to convict if the speech "stirs public anger, invites dispute, or brings about a condition of unrest." The Supreme Court deemed that instruction an error in violation of the First Amendment and thus a conviction based on those grounds would not stand. In *R.A.V. v. City of St. Paul*, a 1992 case dealing with the constitutionality of a cross-burning statute, the Supreme Court said that fighting words are not protected speech because of their non-speech elements. Fighting words are "analogous to a noisy sound truck,"[20] the court said; it is the noise caused by fighting words that warrants regulation. The Supreme Court ruled that the government may not regulate the use of fighting words based on hostility or favoritism toward the underlying message, because the First Amendment prohibits limiting speech on the basis of the viewpoint being communicated. That case also serves as a reminder that content-based regulations must meet the threshold of strict scrutiny, which requires the government to demonstrate a compelling interest and for the regulation to be narrowly drawn. Thus, courts have found hate speech statutes that fail to follow the narrow definition of fighting words to be unconstitutional.

"Incitement to violence" refers to expression that calls on bystanders to engage in immediate violent action. To be considered unprotected incitement to violence under the *Brandenberg* test, speech must be "directed to inciting or producing imminent lawless action" and be "likely to produce such action." To bring an effective charge, there must be a specific and immediate call to violence. William White, a White supremacist, received a three-year jail sentence for using his website, www.overthrow.com, to incite violence against the jury foreman in a trial of another neo-Nazi.[21] In this instance, a judge said that posting the jury foreman's name, address, and phone numbers online was considered incitement to illegal activity, and White was found guilty and his conviction was upheld on appeal. Notably, the imminence standard can be particularly difficult to meet in cases involving online content because of the difficulty proving that a particular website or social media post caused an individual to engage in an illegal action.

Finally, "true threats" encompass "those statements where the speaker means to communicate a serious expression of an intent to commit an act of unlawful violence to a particular individual or group of individuals." In the case of *Virginia v. Black*, the Supreme Court considered whether a state's cross-burning statute was permissible, and Justice Sandra Day O'Connor joined four other justices in allowing states to ban cross burning carried out with the intent to intimidate. The court said that Virginia may choose to regulate this subset of intimidating messages in light of cross burning's long and pernicious history as a signal of impending violence.

Although the Supreme Court did not carve out the true threats exception for Virginia's cross-burning statute until 2003, in the late 1990s, Congress adopted a law that articulates the elements of a true threat. Since then, there have been a handful of successful prosecutions of individuals who create and disseminate threats, either in person or online. For example, in 2001 the US Circuit Court of Appeals for the Fifth Circuit upheld an 18-year-old high school student's guilt for making true threats when he repeatedly said in an internet chat room that he planned to kill other students at his school, and gave no indication he was joking. In order to support a conviction like this under the true threats statute, the government must prove three elements of the crime: a transmission in interstate or foreign commerce, a communication containing a threat, and a threat to injure or kidnap the person of another. Specifically, the US Code states, "whoever transmits in interstate or foreign commerce any communication containing any threat to kidnap any person or any threat to injure the person of another, shall be fined under this title or imprisoned not more than five years, or both." Cases regarding a violation of this statute often fail to meet the threshold of a direct threat to injure or kidnap an individual. In their application of this law, courts have considered the extent to which the threat is believable—an essential determinant of whether or not an utterance or expression should be considered a true threat.

Recently, the Supreme Court had a chance to reconcile the true threats doctrine from *Virginia v. Black* with the existing federal statutes, and demonstrate its application to threatening posts made on social media. However, the court chose not to do this. In *Elonis v. United States*, the Supreme Court took up the question of whether or not a conviction requires proof of the defendant's subjective intent to threaten. In an 8–1 decision, the court held that the prosecution needed to show that the person posting the threats actually *intended* to threaten another person. Thus, Elonis had to be aware of his actions to threaten another person in order to be convicted for making an illegal threat.

In the United States, there are very few options for victims seeking damages for the harm caused by individuals who engage in hate speech. While many other countries recognize the tort of "group defamation," the identification standard used by most states in the United States only recognizes defamatory statements made to small groups or individuals as harmful. Therefore, comments aimed at entire ethnicities do not qualify as grounds for a successful suit. However, as legal scholar Jeremy Waldron argues, group libel should be considered as a means of recourse for victims.[22] Notably, in *Beauharnais v. Illinois* (1952), the Supreme Court upheld an Illinois group libel statute that declared the distribution of publications that disseminate hate-laden information to be an act of criminal libel, which only some states continue to recognize. However, the logic offered in the *Beauharnais* case is rarely relied upon as the justification for exempting hate speech from First Amendment protection.

Legal theorists Richard Delgado and Jean Stefancic have also advocated for a civil action for racially insulting language under the intentional infliction of emotional distress tort.[23] The question here is whether the victims of hate speech can successfully claim that they have suffered emotional harm. Thus far, the answer from the Supreme Court has been a resounding "no." In *Snyder v. Phelps* (2011), Albert Snyder sued members of the Westboro Baptist Church, including Fred W. Phelps, for Intentional Infliction of Emotional Distress (IIED), Intrusion Upon Seclusion, and Civil Conspiracy for protesting the funeral of his son, Marine Lance Corporal Matthew Snyder, with signs that said, "F*gs Doom Nations," "Thank God for Dead Soldiers," and "Priests Rape Boys." Although a Maryland jury had returned a verdict in favor of Snyder on three claims, including IIED, the Supreme Court found, in an 8–1 decision, that the First Amendment shields Westboro from tort liability because the speech was a matter of public concern and happened in a public place.

Although the United States treats hate speech differently from many countries, when it comes to liability for online intermediaries, the United States is in lockstep with the United Nations, the European Union, and most other nations. In the United States, social media organizations and other ISPs are not liable for the content shared by users on their sites. The Communications Decency Act (CDA) absolves ISPs of the responsibility to police content on their site for fear of the chilling effect it may create. Part of the Telecommunications Act of 1996, the CDA held that indecent and obscene material should be regulated in cyberspace. Although the indecency portion of the law was struck down in *Reno v. ACLU*, the Supreme Court upheld Section 230 of the act because they interpreted it to mean that operators of internet services are not to be construed as publishers and, therefore, are not legally liable for the words of third parties who use their services. The court said that any law requiring ISPs to restrict or eliminate speech to avoid liability would create an "obvious chilling effect" on speech.

Despite the *Reno* verdict, in 2018, Congress passed two pieces of legislation that run directly counter to the court's logic for protecting Section 230. The "Allow States to Fight Online Sex Trafficking Act" and the "Stop Enabling Sex Traffickers Act," which are collectively known as

FOSTA/SESTA, create exceptions to Section 230 which increase civil and criminal liabilities for websites hosting ads for "prostitution." With the exception of FOSTA/SESTA, the United States takes an essentially hands-off approach to internet content regulation.

The lack of legal prohibitions against hate speech in the United States has allowed hateful expression to flourish. In 2018, the Southern Poverty Law Center identified 1,020 active hate groups in the country, many of which have their own websites and social media pages. A 2017 study by the Pew Research Center for Internet and Technology found that approximately one in ten Americans had been harassed online because of their race, ethnicity, or gender. Notably, one in four African Americans said they had been targeted online because of their race or ethnicity, as had one in ten Hispanics.[24] Hate speech proliferates in public discourse across the United States. Swastikas show up on synagogues and many people use racist, misogynistic, and homophobic slurs in casual conversation without fear of any legal repercussions.

Conclusion

From international directives to cooperative efforts with tech companies, to criminal sanctions with fines and jail time, to civil remedies, there are many different ways to prohibit and/or punish hate speech. What is missing from this equation is comprehensive data regarding outcomes. Unfortunately, no single measurement can determine the impact each of these efforts is having. Instead, scholars and researchers rely on a combination of quantitative, qualitative, and anecdotal data to paint a picture of how various approaches to regulation influence people's use of hate speech, both in person and online.

The European Commission's decision to work with tech companies to review and remove any illegal hate speech has been effective in reducing the amount of this content that appears online. Germany's strong criminal sanctions also work to limit hate speech, but have failed to prevent biased, authoritarian perspectives from gaining a renewed foothold in the country. Japan acted quickly to establish laws that express disdain for hate speech directed at certain groups, but not others. Brazil has both criminal and civil penalties associated with hate speech, but hate speech continues to be prevalent in the country and the country's current president is making it more common. South Africa has instituted strong prohibitions against hate speech with jail time, but often these rules have been used against members of groups who are already oppressed. Canada has comprehensive laws against hate speech, but still struggles to find the right balance between the right to free expression, the right to religious freedom, and the need to protect human dignity. Canada is also one among many countries struggling to determine whether and how religious freedom should be protected, particularly when the content of religious expression is denigrating to others. Meanwhile, in the United States, there are almost no prohibitions against hate speech, unless it crosses the line into incitement of immediate violence or threatens a person's physical well-being. Unlike several of the countries examined, the United States places the right to free expression above many others and does not recognize a legal right to human dignity, which is the first article in the United Nations Universal Declaration of Human Rights. Other countries, such as Canada, place an individual's right to dignity, which describes the right to be valued, respected, and treated ethically simply for being human, above the right to free expression. For most countries, the goal is to balance the right to dignity with an individual's right to express herself or himself freely.

In the United States, the right to free expression is almost absolute and may only be curtailed in certain instances, such as when the expression itself threatens national security or contains obscenity. This approach, with its narrow categories of exception to near-absolute protection, also raises serious questions about how countries are characterizing incitement. In the United States, laws focus on short-term incitement to criminal acts. However, in other countries, such as Canada, courts have recognized the role of hate speech in laying the groundwork for later attacks on vulnerable groups, which can range from discrimination to segregation to genocide. The way different countries recognize hate speech varies depending on their collective views regarding whether and how hate speech harms individuals and society as a whole. Libel laws in the United States provide recourse for individuals whose reputations are harmed by false statements, whereas in Germany, false statements made about entire groups of people may be punished.

Several issues about hate speech regulation are raised by this analysis, including:

• the complex balancing act required for countries to simultaneously respect human dignity and freedom of expression;

• the difficulty establishing laws that protect all people, such as women and members of the LGBTQIA community;

• the tension surrounding religious expression that is hateful or discriminatory toward members of a particular group;

• the very real concerns about hate speech laws being used to silence important political dissent; and

• the lack of responsibility currently placed on online platforms.

The way different countries recognize hate speech varies depending on their collective views regarding whether and how hate speech harms individuals and society as a whole.

However, the good news is, people are trying. Across the globe, countries and international bodies are working to minimize short-term and, in some cases, long-term incitement to hatred based on a person's identity characteristics. Legislative bodies are working to craft laws that respect human dignity while upholding an individual's right to freedom of expression. As the French sociologist Emile Durkheim said, courts use criminal sanctions to mark the boundary between what is acceptable and unacceptable in public life.[25] While there are still many questions to be answered about the impacts of various regulatory approaches and even the relationship between hate speech and bias-motivated violence, the good news is that most countries, with the exception of the United States, have designated hate speech as something that should be considered unacceptable in public life.

CURRENT ISSUES: HATE SPEECH ON US COLLEGE CAMPUSES

In 2017, College Republicans invited former Breitbart News editor and political provocateur Milo Yiannopoulos to speak at the University of Washington. Yiannopoulos, who has since been banned from both Twitter and Facebook for using hate speech, is known for his disparaging comments about Muslims, the transgender community, and other marginalized groups. He visited the University of Washington as part of a nationwide tour of college campuses which he embarked on to promote free speech and to "educate" students about bad ideas, including progressive social justice, the Black Lives Matter movement, and feminism. During his one-hour talk to about 200 students at the University of Washington, Yiannopoulos criticized progressives, feminists, and academics that condemn hate speech. Protests at the event eventually turned violent, and one protester was shot in the stomach.

When Yiannopoulos was slated to speak at the University of California, Berkeley, during the same tour, antifascist activists known as "antifa" protested the event by tearing down barricades, shooting projectiles at police, and setting fires. Their actions caused $100,000 worth of damage and the school made a decision to cancel the speech, citing safety concerns.

Less than a year later, the Unite the Right Rally took place on the University of Virginia's campus. In August 2017, White nationalists marched on campus and in the adjacent town of Charlottesville, chanting slogans such as "Jews will not replace us." James Alex Fields Jr. deliberately drove his car into a crowd of counterprotestors, killing Heather Heyer. Fields has since been sentenced to life in prison as punishment for her murder.

These incidents, and others like them, raise questions about the potentially violent consequences of allowing hate speech on college campuses. As we discussed in the previous chapter, the United States permits hate speech, provided it does not cross the line into incitement, true threats, or fighting words. As a result, hate speech has emerged in a variety of forms across college campuses over the past few decades. This includes hate speech used by invited speakers, as well as expression that takes place between students, and between students and faculty, during class or at campus events. Even monuments or mascots on college campuses have been construed as hateful. Graffiti

Figure 5 Neo-Nazis prepare to march during the Unite the Right Rally at the University of Virginia in 2017. *Source:* CC BY 2.0.

and flyers that promote a White supremacist ideology regularly appear on college campuses. According to BuzzFeed News, there were at least 154 recorded incidents of hate speech on US college campuses between November 2016 and September 2017.[1]

Historically, bias-motivated violence and political dissent have both flourished on college campuses. In the 1990s, not long before the genocide of eight hundred thousand Tutsis by Hutus, Hutu student groups targeted

Tutsi students on Rwandan college campuses. Before the Holocaust, university fraternities in Germany openly disparaged Jewish citizens, spreading anti-Semitic slogans like "Jews are our misfortune." Dialectically, students at university campuses have also been at the center of important political movements, such as the protests against the Vietnam War and, more recently, Black Lives Matter, both of which could have potentially been stymied if campus administrators were in a position to restrict student expression. Colleges and universities play a dual role as institutions of higher learning and places where people work and live, which raises difficult questions about how hate speech should be handled.

Protecting Hate Speech on US College Campuses

In the United States, the First Amendment protects expression in informal settings, such as the university quad, much the same way it allows for most expression on public sidewalks and streets. In fact, the federal funding received by public colleges establishes a public forum, which prevents administrators and students from restricting speech supported by those funds based on its content. In the 1970s, the Supreme Court ruled that the mere dissemination of ideas on a university campus, no matter how offensive to good taste, may not be shut off only in the name

Colleges and universities play a dual role as institutions of higher learning and places where people work and live, which raises difficult questions about how hate speech should be handled.

of "conventions of decency."[2] Then, in 2000, the Supreme Court concluded that universities have an obligation to create and maintain a public forum for debate, in response to student protestors who objected to their activity fees funding ideological objectives they opposed.[3]

The judiciary's position on free expression prevents campus administrators from controlling the content of student press outlets, but also designates speech codes prohibiting hate speech as unconstitutional. In the 1980s, universities in the United States began adopting and strengthening campus hate speech codes. However, courts have consistently held that statutes punishing offensive or unseemly speech are unconstitutionally overbroad. In two separate cases, courts ruled that hate speech codes, which prohibited the use of racist or discriminatory comments to demean others based on race, gender, or sexual orientation, were too vague and could not be considered a reasonable extension of the fighting words doctrine.[4] In their book, *Free Speech on Campus*, legal scholars Erwin Chemerinsky and Howard Gillman argue that hate speech codes should be avoided so that people are not punished for their political views. The authors also recognize that hate speech codes may be discriminatorily enforced and used to punish the speech of people who are not the intended targets.[5] For example, during the year when the University of Michigan's speech code was enforced, more than 20 African American students were charged with racist speech against White students, while not a single instance of racist speech by Whites was punished.[6]

While hate speech codes are generally considered unconstitutional, professional standards can often restrict student speech. For example, the University of Minnesota sanctioned a student for a satirical commentary about a cadaver based on rules directly related to professional standards.[7] The University of Hawaii denied another student a student-teacher placement based on comments made in class about students with disabilities and sexual relationships with children.[8]

In the classroom and other formal settings, such as the library or university events, students and professors can be held to professional and pedagogical standards, but those same rules do not apply in informal spaces.[9] Educators, like employers, can require students and employees to refrain from sexually harassing speech or harassment based on race, ethnicity, sexual orientation, etc. in order to maintain equal educational opportunities. Title IV of the Civil Rights Act prohibits institutions receiving federal funds from establishing a hostile environment where harassing conduct (physical, verbal, graphic, or written) is severe, pervasive, or persistent enough to interfere with an individual's ability to participate in or benefit from the services, activities, or privileges provided by the recipient of the funds. However, the Office of Civil Rights distinguishes between harassment and offensive speech regarding sex, race, disability, etc. Expression including words and symbols is permitted, whereas conduct such as harassment, which keeps students from participating and benefiting from an educational program, is prohibited.

Parsing the line between hate speech and harassment can be difficult. In 2016, students from Texas A&M taunted a group of African American high school students from the Uplift Hampton Preparatory School in Dallas during a campus visit. Students yelled racial slurs at the visiting high schoolers, told them to "go back where they came from," and one woman asked if the high school students liked her confederate flag earrings. University police interviewed several of the individuals involved, but did not file formal charges. One of the university students is reportedly no longer associated with the school, but details beyond that were not released because of student privacy concerns.

Hate speech like this on US college campuses can take many forms. It can include the use of racial or other epithets, like the incident at Texas A&M, but it can also escalate to illegal harassment. Universities' existing policies often navigate between protecting expression and prohibiting discrimination. Many of these draw on language from relevant First Amendment doctrine or anti-discrimination laws. The University of Idaho maintains rules that prohibit "persistent, severe verbal abuse, threats, intimidation, harassment, coercion, bullying, derogatory comments, vandalism, or other conduct that threatens or endangers the mental or physical health or safety of any person or causes reasonable apprehension of such harm." However, the school says that a single incident of offensive language, including racial epithets, does not violate its rules. The University of Wisconsin's Code of Conduct maintains a commitment and respect for human dignity and pulls language from anti-discrimination law to describe its position on harassment. The University of California, Berkeley, student code of conduct uses language from the existing true threats doctrine to prohibit what it calls terrorizing conduct.[10]

Unlike federally funded public universities, private schools and colleges are free to create whatever approach to free expression they feel is best for their students. Some of these schools, such as Georgetown University, have developed speech and expression policies designed to mimic the rules at public universities. Others, such as Seattle University, where I teach, expressly prohibit bias-related conduct, which includes both language and behaviors that demonstrate bias against people or groups because of race, color, ethnicity, religion, faith, national origin, political orientation, or sexual orientation.

This brief review of existing policies shows that while hate speech codes are considered unconstitutional in the United States, universities may adopt narrowly tailored policies that follow First Amendment and anti-discrimination laws. To be considered constitutional, these policies may not regulate the specific content of student expression but instead must focus on behavior by restricting *conduct* that threatens, harasses, or in some way jeopardizes the safety of other students.

Given that these policies do not directly ban the use of hate speech, the question remains, what are the impacts of permitting hate speech on US college campuses, and how are students, faculty, and administrators responding to this reality?

Microaggressions, Safe Spaces, and Trigger Warnings

While universities struggle to strike a balance between protecting free expression and preventing student harm, historically, college campuses have not welcomed individuals with marginalized identities. In addition to hate speech, students with marginalized identities must also deal with "microaggressions," which are verbal, nonverbal, or environmental slights or insults based on discriminatory belief systems that communicate (intentionally or unintentionally) hostile, derogatory, or negative messages about those targeted. Microaggressions can take many forms. Often, faculty single out students to represent the viewpoint of their entire racial or ethnic group. Students also commit microaggressions toward one another in a variety of ways. For example, a White student singing along to music that contains the N-word might be offensive to students of color, as would asking an Asian student for help with homework because of their race, or asking someone with a darker skin tone where they're "really from."

US colleges and universities have traditionally been primarily White, hetero-normative spaces, which can make learning and thriving difficult for students with marginalized identities. In response to these conditions, students and administrators have created "safe spaces," designated environments in which students can explore ideas and express themselves in a context with well-understood ground rules for conversations. "Trigger warnings" are also used to let students know that upcoming material may be upsetting for some. For example, a professor may give a trigger or content warning before discussing a text that includes sexual assault, allowing students who may be uncomfortable with the discussion to exit the room.

Politicians, parents, professors, and university administrators have spoken out about the use of trigger warnings. Former President Barack Obama said that young people do not need to be coddled or protected from different points of view. He believes that if someone with whom students disagree comes to campus, they should have an argument with them, not silence them. College, Obama said, should be a place for students to widen their horizons and make them better citizens, and the way to do that is to create a space where lots of ideas are presented.[11] By arguing about and testing different theories, students must consider their own, sometimes narrow, points of view.

President Trump's administration has gone so far as to issue an executive order regarding free speech on college campuses, reminding universities not to illegally police speech based on its content. This order was likely issued in response to the idea, popular among the political right, that liberal ideas are securing a foothold in US universities while conservative voices are being drowned out. For example, the Young America's Foundation canceled a talk by conservative pundit Ann Coulter at the University of California, Berkeley, over fears that protests against her speech would turn violent. At Middlebury College in Vermont, students shouted down a discussion between one of their professors and Charles Murray, an author and political scientist whose books argue that marginalized groups are disadvantaged because they cannot compete with intellectually, psychologically, and morally superior White men. First Amendment scholars call this technique of shouting down a speaker the "Heckler's Veto," and many view it as another form of censorship.

In 2016, John Ellison, dean of students at the University of Chicago, directly addressed the issue in a letter to the incoming freshmen class that said intellectual safe spaces and trigger warnings would no longer exist on campus, and controversial speakers would no longer be canceled. A

CBS News Special interviewed students at the University of Chicago who received this letter. Junior Mary Blair, an African American, said she felt like the letter represented a fundamental misunderstanding of safe spaces and their value and importance in any kind of setting. Eric Wesson, a White law student, responded, "There's a real risk aversion on these campuses. You know, once people enter the real world, I don't think the real world is a safe space." Blair replied, "I can assure you that all people of color who have existed in a primarily white space know that the world is not a safe space."

Misunderstandings about the nature and purpose of safe spaces, microaggressions, and trigger warnings abound. The 2018 book, *The Coddling of the American Mind*, cites safe spaces and trigger warnings as evidence that we now live in a culture in which everyone must think twice before speaking up, lest they face charges of insensitivity, aggression, or worse. The authors, Greg Lukianoff and Jonathan Haidt, argue that higher education has incorrectly taught students that they are fragile, emotional beings, living in a world of good versus evil. This protectiveness toward young people has created a culture of extreme safety that leads to intimidation and violence, like the Unite the Right protests in Charlottesville, VA, or witch hunts against those who speak out about these issues.[12] Likewise, Nadine Strossen, who is the former president of the ACLU and author of *Hate: Why We Should Resist It with*

"I can assure you that all people of color who have existed in a primarily white space know that the world is not a safe space."

Free Speech Not Censorship, argues that restrictions on hate speech are not needed. Instead, counterspeech can be the most valuable way to counteract the harms caused by hate speech.[13] Rather than restricting expression, proponents of this idea believe that what is needed is more speech. If you don't like what an invited speaker has to say, hold a separate event to discuss why those views are incorrect.

According to Lukianoff and Haidt, attempting to shield students from potentially harmful expression amplifies their anxiety and makes it more difficult for them to have open discussions where they practice the skills of critical thinking and civil disagreement. It also poorly prepares them for professional life, which often demands intellectual engagement with people and ideas one might find uncongenial or wrong. Instead, they argue, students should be taught how to live in a world full of potential offenses and should not conflate emotional comfort with physical safety. One way to do this is through cognitive behavioral therapy, which the authors believe to be among the most humane and supportive things a university could provide, given the rising rates of mental illness.

The suggestion at the heart of this argument is that the students themselves must commit to making fundamental changes, learning to better navigate the challenging waters of life and to accept things as they are. People will always say and do things students don't like, so they must learn to deal with it, rather than encouraging them to change their words or behavior. College, the authors argue, is the best environment on earth to learn the lesson that life is not fair and to come face to face with ideas and people who are offensive and even hostile. By this logic, rather than seek to change the rules so that those behaviors and language are prohibited (or at the very least, discouraged), students of color in a classroom should learn to deal with microaggressions or even hate speech used by their White counterparts.

Lukianoff and Haidt also ignore the extent to which language is used to create shared meaning and shape our perceived realities. Hate speech not only maligns an individual based on race, gender, sexual orientation, etc., but also reinforces the dominant social order. The arguments the authors present focus more on the fear of losing the "way things have been" and maintaining the existing social order rather than on any real concern for student learning. Rather than an unwillingness to engage with controversial ideas, shifting attitudes among students toward hate speech and, more broadly, limits to free expression on college campuses may instead represent a greater empathy on the part of young people for people with marginalized identities. For example, a 2015 study by the Pew Research Center found that 40 percent of millennials were OK with limiting speech that was offensive to minorities, while only 24 percent of baby boomers said the government should be able to prevent such speech.[14]

When it comes to invited speakers, the value of giving people like Milo Yiannopoulos a platform to espouse hate speech on campus is questionable at best. As legal scholar and Georgetown University professor Alexander Tsesis has said, hate speakers are generally not inviting intellectual debate or seeking political dialogue, but instead silencing people through intimidation and limiting the marketplace of ideas on college campuses. The goals of democratic self-governance or self-expression do not require that we extend protection to speech that diminishes the sense of security for those targeted and limits their ability to enjoy common areas or attend university-sponsored events on campus.[15]

Scholars take umbrage with the purported value speakers like Milo Yiannopoulos and Charles Murray contribute to the discourse. However, the Engineering Department of a university would never invite the architect who designed the Genoa Bridge in Italy, which collapsed in 2018 and killed 43 people, to speak at a campus event. Why, then, should speakers like Murray, who espouses information that we know to be false, such as the notion that people of color are intellectually or morally inferior to their White counterparts, be given a platform to share his incorrect ideas? As legal scholar W. Bradley Wendel reminds us, people don't have to be skeptical about the truth of every proposition simply because it cannot be verified using the methods of natural science research. There are matters, such as the evils of slavery, segregation, and racial bigotry, about which there is no reasonable disagreement. Failure to act on the part of the university is also a form of action. By doing nothing, the institution indicates its acceptance of the status quo on this issue.

Student Perspectives on Hate Speech

In 2018, College Pulse (funded by the Knight Foundation) conducted a study to measure student attitudes toward hate speech on campus. They surveyed a total of 4,407 full-time college students enrolled in four-year degree programs, revealing that 58 percent of students agreed that hate speech, which they defined as "attacks on people based on their race, religion, gender identity, or sexual orientation," should be protected by the First Amendment, while 41 percent of students disagreed with that statement.[16] Differences in perceptions varied based on an individual's race, gender, and sexual orientation. For example, 60 percent of African American college students agreed that promoting an inclusive society that welcomes diverse groups was more important than protecting free speech, while 58 percent of White students said that free expression should be the priority. A majority of college women (53 percent) said that hate speech should not be protected by the First Amendment. However, 74 percent of college men said hate speech should remain protected under the First Amendment. Views on this issue also varied significantly by sexual orientation. Nearly two-thirds (64 percent) of heterosexual students say that hate speech should be protected, while only 35 percent of gay and lesbian college students agreed. More than half of White students (53 percent) said it is never acceptable to try to prevent controversial speakers from expressing their views on campus, while fewer Hispanic (41 percent), African American (38 percent), and Asian Pacific Islander students (37 percent) agreed. Nearly two-thirds of White male students (65 percent) said shouting down speakers was never acceptable, compared to 45 percent of White women polled.

This data draws attention to the stark differences between how White students and students of color view these issues, as well as differences between how men and women and gay and straight students perceive freedom of expression and hate speech on college campuses in the United States. Notably, those who are less likely to be victims of hate speech are more likely to allow it compared to students who have been targeted. This study demonstrates that perspectives on protecting hate speech are changing. If 40 percent of college students are in favor of limiting speech to protect dignity, we may eventually see a change in US jurisprudence regarding hate speech. For now, though, public colleges and universities are left to find a balance between protecting free expression and preventing harm to students.

Navigating Between Hate Speech and Free Speech

In a recent case, the Supreme Court struck down the government's choice not to issue a trademark it deemed racially offensive. In that decision, the Supreme Court held that the proudest boast of our free speech jurisprudence is that we protect the freedom to express "the thought we hate."[17] Legal scholars Richard Delgado and Jean Stefancic have pointed out that this legal narrative is at odds with current public norms. Hate speech is generally condemned, except by our legal system. Delgado and Stefancic believe the United States would benefit from discarding legal formalism in favor of legal realism, which would take things like history, social science, economics, and policy into account. They call on judges to recognize their own implicit bias around these issues:

> The formalistic, clipped jurisprudence in this area
> is ironic because the First Amendment supposedly
> protects and encourages a full debate of important
> public issues. But with campus hate speech, as with
> free speech in general, it does not. It assures exactly
> the opposite: cliché-ridden argumentation and

judicial opinions that give scant attention to valid arguments that the other side may be advancing, and even less to social science, political science, history, or the demands of an emerging multiracial, multicultural society.[18]

Delgado and Stefancic also characterize US hate speech cases as backward-looking and at odds with campus administrators who generally try to create campus atmospheres where all students feel welcome and safe enough to engage in the robust exchange of views that a successful college education demands. As Morton Shapiro, president of Northwestern University, said, "I'm an economist, not a sociologist or psychologist, but those experts tell me that students don't fully embrace uncomfortable learning unless they themselves are comfortable."[19] The unchecked use of hate speech has the power to silence those targeted. Therefore, if US colleges and universities aim to truly establish an environment where all students can wrestle with difficult ideas, then there must be some ground rules that allow individuals to feel safe enough to engage in that process.

Exploring Solutions

In his book, *Safe Spaces, Brave Places*, educator John Palfrey says that diversity and free expression can and should

"Students don't fully embrace uncomfortable learning unless
they themselves are comfortable."

coexist because both principles are required to establish equity and fairness among students.[20] Palfrey echoes the recommendations of the National Association of Student Personnel Administrators, who have called for "brave spaces" to be formed alongside safe spaces on US college campuses.[21] NASPA characterizes brave spaces as classroom environments in which students:

1. civilly engage in controversy;

2. own their intentions and impacts; openly discuss when and where dialogue has affected the emotional well-being of another person;

3. engage in challenge by choice: students have the option to step in and out of challenging conversations;

4. are respectful; and

5. avoid attacks.

This approach acknowledges the silencing effect that the unchecked use of hate speech can have on classroom discussions. As Palfrey argues, there are ways to protect students from the harm of hate speech, while also safeguarding their right to free expression. For example, narrowly tailored speech codes can be used to prohibit threats, harassment, and incitement. Campuses can also establish different expectations for student expression that takes place in private spaces, like dorm rooms, and public spaces, like the university quad.

Nadine Strossen's call for more speech is also useful for universities seeking to foster a sense of community and raise awareness about the impacts of microaggressions and implicit bias. In addition, counterspeech can be used to combat the negative impacts of having controversial speakers on campus. When controversial speakers like Milo Yiannopoulos are invited to campus, universities can hold alternative events for students to participate in. Students can also show up to peacefully protest the ideas being espoused by the speaker. Regardless of the specific approach taken, universities benefit when they are proactive about how to best address issues associated with hate speech, respecting students' right to free expression while considering the needs of students from traditionally marginalized groups.

CURRENT ISSUES: HATE SPEECH AND SOCIAL MEDIA

In recent decades, hate speech has found a new place to proliferate—social media. Social networking sites have made every user a publisher who can broadcast his or her views to the world. Combined with the anonymity of the internet, social media sites have created an environment where hate speech can flourish. In a 2017 survey, one in ten Americans said they had been harassed online because of their race, ethnicity, or gender. One in four African Americans said they had been targeted online because of their race or ethnicity, as had one in ten Hispanics.[1] Hate speech appears on Facebook, Instagram, Twitter, YouTube, and nearly every other social media platform on the internet. Although there are no formal counts of hate speech on social media globally, Facebook's

In recent decades, hate speech has found a new place to proliferate—social media.

transparency report indicated that during the first quarter of 2020, the company took action on 9.6 million pieces of content.

The hateful words, images, and symbols posted on social media can have severe impacts on society, as well as on individuals. Hate speech on social media spreads stereotypes, creates emotional and psychological harm to those targeted, and often has a silencing effect on online discourse. A recent study showed how offensive Facebook pages manipulated by Danish citizens to look like those of radical Islamic groups provoked negative sentiment toward Muslims in Denmark.[2] Social media content has also been tied to several incidents of bias-motivated violence. For example, the shooter in the 2018 Tree of Life Synagogue massacre in Pittsburgh was a participant on the social media platform Gab, which is home to extremists who have been banned by larger platforms. There, he posted conspiracy theories about Jewish people, claiming that they were working to render White people as minorities in the United States. The perpetrator of the 2019 mass shooting in El Paso, Texas, which left 22 people dead and 24 injured, posted a four-page document to the site 8chan that included White nationalist and racist propaganda, and blamed immigrants for stealing Americans' jobs.

Figure 6 These comments were posted to a story on Sarah Palin's Facebook page about Rep. Ilhan Omar, a Muslim American woman elected to Congress in 2018.

In addition to fueling stereotypes and building negative (mis)perceptions of certain groups, online hate speech has very real impacts on individuals. As Jessie Daniels's work has shown, the internet affords a space for identity construction around race and ethnicity.[3] Perhaps the worst impact these negative messages have is that people will come to believe the things said about them in social media content and to believe in their own inferiority.[4] Critical race scholars see hate speech as a form of assault, which harms those targeted.[5]

The existence of hate speech on social media may also have a silencing effect on the expression and political participation of women, people of color, and LGBTQIA folks. Danielle Keats Citron and Helen Norton have developed a theory of digital citizenship, which refers to the various ways that online activities deepen civic engagement, political participation, and public conversation.[6] Citron argues that individuals targeted by online hate speech cannot participate in their online networks when they are under assault from a barrage of gendered or other slurs.[7] In a 2016 editorial for the *Washington Post*, Vijaya Gadde, Twitter's general counsel, acknowledged that freedom of expression would mean little as an underlying philosophy for the company if they continued to allow voices to be silenced because people were afraid to speak up.

This chapter will explore the problem of hate speech on social media and look at how social media organizations' efforts to regulate this content can impact freedom of expression for their users and shape the larger universe of discourse around these issues. To begin, I will outline the legal guidelines social media companies must follow. Next, we'll look at their content moderation policies and procedures in order to understand what platforms are doing to regulate hate speech and whether or not it is working. I will demonstrate how hate speech in social media can fuel stereotypes and create the conditions for violence. Finally, we'll explore potential solutions for minimizing the amount of content containing hate speech that exists on social media and consider potential issues associated with this type of censorship.

Legal Framework

With the exception of Germany, countries and international governing bodies such as the United Nations or the European Union do not generally believe social media companies should be liable for what users say on their sites. Instead, their established laws prohibit and punish the individuals that create or disseminate this content online, not holding the social media companies themselves responsible for what users do on their platforms.

Although hate speech is legal in the United States, social media organizations are considered private virtual spaces and thus are not required to extend First Amendment protection to the content created and shared on their platforms. The terms of service that users sign act as a contract between an individual and a company such as Twitter or YouTube. To retain the privilege of posting on a particular site, users must adhere to the community guidelines set by the social media organization. Platforms may discipline users that violate community standards or terms of service by removing offending content or accounts. However, the US government will rarely intervene. Section 230 of the Communications Decency Act (CDA) states that providers of interactive computer services in the United States, such as ISPs or social media companies, shall not be treated as publishers and, therefore, are not responsible for what third parties do on their sites.

While the United States takes an essentially hands-off approach to the regulation of hate speech in social media content, in 2017, Germany passed the Network Enforcement Law, or NetzDG, which requires social media companies with more than two million users to remove or block access to reported content that violates restrictions against hate speech included in the German Criminal Code. Companies must remove "obvious hate speech" within 24 hours of receiving a notification or risk a €50 million fine. Proponents of this law believe it is necessary in order to motivate companies like Facebook, Twitter, and others to act more aggressively to stem the tide of hate flowing from their sites. Those who disagree with the law feel it goes too far in limiting expression and will likely result in the removal of what should be considered legal and permitted content on these sites. Following Germany's lead, in July 2019, France's National Assembly passed a law requiring social media networks to remove obviously hateful content or risk a fine of up to €1.4 million. The law also requires social media sites to create a new button to make it easier for users to report abuse.

In addition to creating legal parameters to address hate speech on social media, many governments have established cooperative agreements with social media companies to address the issue. After the 2019 attack on two mosques in New Zealand, global leaders met with executives from Facebook, Google, Twitter, and other companies to compile a set of guidelines called the "Christchurch Call," which sought to enact measures against extreme, violent, and hateful rhetoric online. Notably, the United States did not sign the pledge. The European Commission is currently working directly with social media organizations including Facebook, Twitter, and YouTube to combat the spread of hateful content in Europe. In May 2016, the group presented a Code of Conduct on Countering Illegal Hate Speech Online. A February 2019 report indicated that since the implementation of the Code of Conduct, "IT companies are now assessing 89 percent of flagged content within 24 hours and 72 percent of the content deemed to be illegal hate speech is removed, compared to 40 percent and 28 percent respectively when the code was first launched in 2016."[8] In the United States, Facebook, Google, Microsoft, and Twitter have partnered with the Anti-Defamation League (ADL) to create a Cyberhate Problem-Solving Lab to address the growing tide of online hate.

Despite these efforts to reduce the volume of hate speech on social media, the problem persists. In order to understand why, we must take a detailed look at the process of content moderation to see what social media companies are doing and whether those efforts are working.

Content Moderation

Content moderation is best defined as a series of practices with shared characteristics which are used to screen user-generated content to determine what will make it onto or remain on a social media platform. This process often includes three distinct phases: editorial review, automatic detection, and community flagging.[9] Social media organizations regulate all kinds of potentially harmful content, including hate speech, violence or incitement, adult nudity, sexual exploitation of adults, sexual solicitation, suicide/self-injury, bullying/harassment, child nudity, privacy violations, image privacy rights, promoting crime, or selling regulated goods. Here, we'll look specifically at how social media companies engage in content moderation of hate speech.

Editorial Review

Editorial review, the first phase in the process of content moderation, imposes oversight on content before it is made available, such as the ratings given to movies prior to their release.[10] In the case of social media, editorial review often refers to the community standards set by social media platforms. Each platform writes and enforces these standards differently, partly because they often operate under slightly different definitions of what qualifies as hate speech–some even use different terms to identify this kind of discourse, including "hate speech," "hateful conduct," "malicious speech," and "hateful imagery." When a social media organization identifies what kind of content qualifies as hate speech, there are generally two parts to the platform's definition: (1) the intention behind the biased words published by a user, and (2) the specific "protected categories" of people who must be targeted by the biased content in order for the post to be removed.

For example, Facebook defines hate speech as "a direct attack on people" based on race, ethnicity, national origin, religious affiliation, sexual orientation, caste, sex, gender, gender identity, serious disease or disability, and immigration status. Facebook defines an attack as "violent or dehumanizing speech." In their community standards, Facebook provides examples of dehumanizing speech, which include comparisons to animals or insects. Statements of physical, mental, or moral inferiority about a group or person because of their identity characteristics also qualify as hate speech under Facebook's rules. Facebook considers calls to exclude or segregate a person or group based on their identity characteristics to be hate speech. The company also labels racial, ethnic, misogynistic, and homophobic slurs as hate speech. At the end of their policy, Facebook notes that criticism of immigration policies and arguments for restricting those policies are allowed, along with humor and social commentary related to these topics.

While Facebook prohibits hate speech, Twitter's community standards ban "hateful conduct" and "hateful imagery and display names." Twitter forbids users from promoting violence or threatening others based on their race, ethnicity, national origin, sexual orientation, gender, gender identity, religious affiliation, age, disability, or serious disease. The company says it does not allow accounts whose primary purpose is to incite harm to others based on this category. The use of the terms "incite" and "threat" are clear nods to the existing categories of speech exempted from First Amendment protection. Twitter, which is generally more protective of speech than Facebook or YouTube, focuses specifically on attacks that include violent threats, wish serious harm on others, reference mass murder or violence toward protected groups, incite violence, or include the repeated use of slurs, epithets, or racist or sexist tropes. Under these rules, a single use of a slur or racist epithet is not enough to violate Twitter's policy. Finally, Twitter addresses hateful imagery directly.

YouTube's community standards indicate that hate speech is not allowed on the site. The company says it will remove content that promotes violence or hatred against individuals or groups based on any of the following attributes: age, caste, disability, ethnicity, gender identity, nationality, race, immigration status, religion, sex/gender, sexual orientation, victims of a major violent event and their kin, or veteran status. YouTube specifically prohibits videos or comments that encourage violence or threaten individuals or groups based on the attributes listed in their policy. Like Twitter, YouTube also specifically prohibits content that incites hatred based on protected categories of identity. YouTube's community standards provide several examples of content that violates their policy, including dehumanizing speech that refers to people or groups as subhuman or compares them to animals, insects, or pests. Content that glorifies violence against protected groups, uses racial, ethnic, religious, or other slurs, or employs stereotypes that incite hatred are all prohibited. YouTube also bans content that claims individuals or groups are mentally inferior, calls for subjugation, or denies violent, well-documented events, such as the Holocaust. Finally, YouTube's community standards note that hate speech can take the form of speech, text, or imagery.

Clearly, social media sites vary on whom they consider to be part of a protected category. Facebook, Twitter, and YouTube all agree that protected categories should include race, ethnicity, religion, sexual orientation, gender, gender identity, and disability. However, not all social media platforms prohibit hate speech targeting people based on age, disease, immigration status, and veteran status. The inconsistency between social media platforms can cause confusion, as one may protect an individual identity from hate speech, while another will not. For example, Facebook and YouTube find comparisons to animals or insects to be hate speech, whereas Twitter does not specifically prohibit this kind of content, instead identifying the repeated use of slurs and hateful imagery as unacceptable hate speech. Likewise, Facebook considers exclusionary language to be hate speech, whereas the other two platforms do not. YouTube is the only platform of these three to specifically prohibit Holocaust denial in their community standards.

Although Facebook, Twitter, YouTube, and other social media sites may all define hate speech differently, they all largely follow the same structure when it comes to enforcing these guidelines. Researchers performed a content analysis of the various responses by platforms when users violate community standards, and found eight possible outcomes that could result from policy violations: account restrictions, sending users warnings, content removal, disabling an account, deleting an account, working with law enforcement, and removal both from search and interface with third parties, which is also referred to as "shadow banning."[11] In the United States, several high-profile members of the alt-right have had their accounts permanently deleted from social media platforms as a result of their continued abuse of the company's policies. Milo Yiannopoulos and conspiracy theorist Alex Jones have both been permanently banned from Twitter. Although rarely invoked, this process of deplatforming is a powerful tool. By removing those who repeatedly and flagrantly ignore a social media organization's community standards, the company effectively takes away their megaphone and makes it far more difficult for these individuals and their ideas to reach a mass audience. Two years after Milo Yiannopoulos was removed from Twitter, he reported continued cancellations of speaking engagements and tour sponsorship, which resulted in a debt of over $4 million.[12]

Social media organizations are sovereign entities able to govern expression on their platforms in whatever way they feel is in the best interest of their users, their advertisers, and their investors. The rules they set via their community standards effectively become the law of the land. Failure to adhere to a platform's community standards can

Social media organizations are sovereign entities able to govern expression on their platforms in whatever way they feel is in the best interest of their users, their advertisers, and their investors.

eliminate an individual's or organization's ability to reach billions of users worldwide.

Automatic Detection

The next phase of content moderation is automatic detection, which utilizes sophisticated software to aid in the content removal process. Platforms use algorithms and/or artificial intelligence to remove content that violates their community standards both before and after it has been uploaded. According to Facebook's First Quarter 2020 Transparency Report, the company proactively removed 89 percent of hate speech on the site before users reported it. Recent research in this area suggests that best practices for algorithms that remove hate speech from social media content are emerging. A 2017 study found that fine-grained labels that help algorithms distinguish between hate speech and merely offensive speech, including humor, were effective.[13] For example, the word f^*g is used in hate speech and offensive language, but the term f^*gg^*t is generally only associated with hate speech. Moreover, posts containing multiple racial or homophobic slurs are more likely to be hate speech, as opposed to offensive language.

While promising, it is important to recognize the extent to which programmers' implicit bias can be infused into the algorithms and artificial intelligence tasked with finding and executing hate speech on social media sites. In her book, *Algorithms of Oppression,* UCLA Associate Professor Safiya Noble explores how racism and sexism can be baked into algorithms for online searches and ad serving.[14] Although she's not looking specifically at social media content moderation, Noble's work suggests that implicit biases are at work when engineers develop the programs that will remove certain forms of hate speech, or not. For example, if an engineer does not see comparisons to animals as a form of hate speech, she may not account for it in her algorithm. This issue highlights the difficulty associated with developing artificial intelligence and algorithms able to distinguish between hate speech prohibited by a platform's community standards and speech that some users may simply find offensive. What appears to be hate speech to an algorithm may in fact be a relatively harmless joke shared between users. This also raises issues regarding who is using particular terms. One woman colloquially referring to a friend as a "bitch" has a far different connotation than a man using that term to refer to a woman.

The high volume of content now being removed by automatic detection also raises concerns about the nature of the posts removed. Facebook, for example, provides no specific details in their transparency reports regarding the content that is being removed. This is particularly troubling given the fact that this expression never has the opportunity to reach the speech marketplace to be seen and considered by users before removal.

Community Flagging

The final, and perhaps most visible, phase of the content moderation process is community flagging, where users report content they believe violates the community standards outlined by the company. Reported content is then manually reviewed by employees who determine whether it will be blocked, deleted, or remain on the site.

There are billions of social media users worldwide and the task of reviewing flagged content is enormous. Facebook users, for example, flag over one million pieces of content worldwide each day.[15] Social media organizations often contract this work out to other organizations such as Upwork, Sutherland, and Deloitte.[16] Workers in these roles are dispersed globally at a variety of worksites, and the work itself often takes place in secret by low-status workers paid very low wages. For example, the median Facebook employee earns $240,000 annually, while a content moderator working for one of these outsourcing companies will earn just $28,800 per year.[17] Workers in these roles suffer panic attacks and other mental health issues as a result of the fifteen hundred violent, hateful, or otherwise troubling posts they review each week. In 2020, Facebook agreed to pay a $52 million settlement to current and former content moderators to compensate for mental health issues developed on the job, including post-traumatic stress disorder. The settlement covers 11,250 content moderators.

In addition to the impacts to their mental health, the lack of pay and prestige assigned to those tasked with reviewing reported posts is problematic. These individuals are responsible for determining whether a piece of reported content is in fact hate speech, or is merely offensive speech. Determining where the line between hate speech and offensive speech lies is an incredibly nuanced form of decision-making that requires both time and training. The low priority given to this process by social media companies like Facebook suggests that the company is perhaps not as concerned as it claims to be about removing expression that incites hatred from their site. A cynical view of this issue would suggest that perhaps Facebook and other social media organizations are happy to leave controversial content, including hate speech, on their site simply because it keeps users engaged with the platform. That prolonged attention can then be translated into advertising dollars.

On a positive note, Facebook is developing and implementing a process for users to adjudicate what they feel are unfair or incorrect decisions regarding content removal. Facebook is creating an oversight board to review controversial content moderation cases. According to the company's draft charter, it plans to create a 40-person global board made up of people appointed by Facebook. It is unclear at this time how many cases the board will review, though the company has said each case will be reviewed by a group of three to five board members who will make a final ruling and provide a public explanation for its decision.[18] Currently, though, there are limited opportunities available to users who wish to challenge a decision made by a platform's content moderators during the review process.

Although social media companies each use a combination of editorial review, automatic detection, and community flagging to police expression on their sites, there are clear issues associated with each phase of the content moderation process that need to be addressed. Community standards should be easy for users to understand and apply. Moreover, the company's response to violations in this process should be uniform so as to avoid claims of prejudice in the application of company policies. The use of artificial intelligence and algorithms to remove content must take into account the implicit bias of software engineers to ensure that the resulting technology is as neutral as possible. Finally, the process of community flagging and subsequent review should be given more prominence within social media companies, considering the important role that content moderators play in distinguishing between hate speech and offensive content.

Perceptions of the Content Moderation Process

Social media users are generally unaware of how the process of content moderation actually works. A study by Sarah

Myers West examined how users interpret the role and function of companies in moderating their content, what kinds of content is taken down, and the impact this has on people's public expression. Myers West's study found that users developed a number of folk theories to explain how and why their content was removed from a platform.[19] Most believed that some form of human intervention—their content being flagged by other users—was the cause, although in reality, algorithms and artificial intelligence play a substantial role in this process. Several users also attributed content removal to a perceived political bias on the part of the company. This may be due, at least in part, to the fact that conservative news sites have more extremely uncivil comments on them. A recent study assessing and comparing the prevalence of incivility in the comments posted on the Facebook pages of American news outlets found that 19 percent of all comments posted on conservative news outlets' Facebook pages were extremely uncivil, compared to 9 percent of comments posted to liberal news outlets' pages.[20] Extremely uncivil comments were also three times as likely to appear on the pages of local news outlets as on national ones.

The perceived bias of social media companies has garnered the attention of President Trump, who has tweeted his dissatisfaction with social media organizations for their perceived bias.

Figure 7 On June 9, 2019, President Trump tweeted about Twitter's decision to ban certain Far Right political pundits for violations of the company's rules.

Trump was reacting to the decision by Facebook and Twitter to ban Far Right conservatives, such as Infowars' Alex Jones, for violating their rules regarding hate speech. The administration has gone so far as to ask social media users to report directly to the White House if they think companies like Facebook and Twitter have wrongly punished them for their political views. President Trump shared an online form to facilitate this process with his Twitter followers in May of 2019.

Social media users' confusion regarding the process of content moderation is unsurprising given the lack of transparency demonstrated by social media organizations around this issue. For example, it wasn't until 2018 that Facebook released a detailed policy update explaining to users how decisions regarding reported hate speech were made. The more clarity platforms can provide to users regarding each phase of the content moderation process—editorial review, automatic detection, and community flagging—the better. As we've seen here, there are opportunities for bias or even simple missteps throughout this process. Educating users will help them follow a platform's stated rules and appropriately challenge decisions if and when mistakes are made.

As this analysis has indicated, social media organizations have enormous power through the process of content moderation to determine which posts, images, and videos reach and remain in the public sphere. Given the role media content plays in shaping dominant ideology around identity characteristics such as race, gender, or sexual orientation, it is essential that social media platforms dedicate the necessary resources to the moderation process.

How Effective Is Content Moderation of Hate Speech?

Despite the extensive efforts taken by social media companies to prohibit and remove hate speech from their sites, an excessive amount of this type of content continues to exist on most social media platforms.

The website NoHomophobes.com, which was created by the Institute for Sexual Minority Studies and Services at the University of Alberta, tracks use of anti-LGBTQIA hate speech on Twitter. It provides a real-time, daily count of the use of slurs, including *f*gg*t* and *d*ke*. In the past five years, the slur *f*gg*t* has been used 40.29 million times and the word *d*ke* has been used 7.5 million times.

My own research into this issue suggests that social media companies have a long way to go toward perfecting the removal process. In a recent study, my coauthor Hayley Rousselle and I identified and reported 311 pieces of content containing hate speech to Facebook and recorded their response.[21] We found that only 47 percent of content we reported was removed. A qualitative analysis of that same content revealed substantial inconsistencies in Facebook's efforts. For example, comparisons of people of color to monkeys or apes were reported twelve times and removed nine of those times. Claims that Muslims were "terrorists" were reported ten times and removed five times. In addition to inconsistencies, Facebook also had trouble removing misogynistic hate speech despite their community standards stating that attacks based on gender will not be tolerated. When reported, hate speech based on gender was removed only 38 percent of the time.

This study also revealed that Facebook had trouble taking context into account during their decision-making process. Several clearly racist or misogynistic comments were not removed, likely because the posts did not contain an actual slur. For example, the phrase "cotton patch b*tch," which was used in a comment regarding Oprah Winfrey, was not removed when it was reported as hate speech. If moderators are unfamiliar with the link between slavery, the history of cotton as a Southern cash crop, and the experience of modern African Americans as the descendants of slaves forced to harvest cotton, then they may not realize how racist this term actually is. These results were unsurprising given the fact that content moderators at Facebook are often expected to review flagged content without being able to see the context in which the comments or posts were made.

In the process of conducting this study, one thing became abundantly clear to my coauthor and me. If we hadn't visited pages like "American White History Month," "Menninst," "Pissed Off White Americans," "The Deplorables," and "Trump 2020," and reported this content, the 48 percent of hate speech that was removed would have likely remained up. This raises questions about the extent to which social media companies are benefiting from and even profiting off hate speech on their sites. Controversial content gets attention and keeps people on the platform longer. This engagement can then be used to guarantee advertisers a certain number of views by their desired demographic. Leaving hate speech up, even after users report it, suggests social media companies may be more interested in profits than people. Facebook, YouTube (which is owned by Google), and Twitter are all publicly traded companies with a fiduciary responsibility to shareholders. Their purpose is to make money. Recognizing Facebook's potential to profit from hate speech, several organizations, including the NAACP, the Anti-Defamation League, and Free Press, worked together to launch the #stophateforprofit campaign, which urged advertisers not to spend money on Facebook advertising during July 2020. The campaign was incredibly successful and convinced more than 1,000 companies, including Starbucks, Target, and Verizon, to stop advertising on Facebook until it makes certain changes such as removing White supremacist groups and participating in a regular audit. Failure on the part of social media companies to act will allow hate speech to continue to propagate, causing severe offline consequences.

Online Hate Speech and Offline Violence

Hate speech on social media has been linked to acts of violence in real life, including mass shootings. For example, the 2012 worldwide release of the anti-Islamic short film, "The Innocence of Muslims," on YouTube sparked demonstrations and violent protests across the globe. Several people were injured and 50 people were killed during these uprisings. The creators of the film, which denigrated the Prophet Muhammad, received several legitimate death threats, and a Pakistani government official offered a bounty for someone to kill the video's producer.

In the United States, perpetrators of recent White supremacist attacks have both consumed and posted hateful content on social media. The Charleston, South Carolina church shooter, who murdered nine African American clergy members during a prayer service at the Emmanuel African Methodist Episcopal Church in 2015, posted photos of himself in a vest featuring White pride symbols to Facebook before the attack. Federal prosecutors in his murder trial indicated that the shooter had been "self-radicalized" through online content and had come to believe that the goal of White supremacy required violent action.

The 2019 attack on two New Zealand mosques, which resulted in the death of 51 people, had several ties to social media. The perpetrator referenced the divisive YouTube star PewDiePie during the attack, and posted his 74 page manifesto to Twitter and 8chan before going on a rampage, which he livestreamed on Facebook and Twitter. Videos of the shooting circulated on Facebook, Reddit, Twitter, and YouTube as the companies scrambled to remove it.

These examples demonstrate the extent to which extremists utilize social media as a tool to spread their message of hate, but even among moderate individuals, hate speech on social media fuels biased perspectives and stereotypes, which can lead to all sorts of mistreatment, from microaggressions to discrimination. Given its wide-ranging negative impacts, it is essential that solutions are identified to curtail the impact of hate speech on social media, while also acknowledging the important role these platforms can play in collective organizing for social change.

Fixing the Problem

With the exception of Germany and France, governments do not hold social media organizations liable for the expression posted on their sites by users. Therefore, social media platforms are largely in a position to regulate themselves. As a result, social media organizations often respond inconsistently to problematic content, which can amplify incendiary rhetoric.

After the murder of George Floyd by Minneapolis police officers, protests against police brutality erupted worldwide. Some demonstrations included violent clashes between police and protesters. Reacting to these events, President Trump tweeted: "These THUGS are dishonoring the memory of George Floyd, and I won't let that happen. Just spoke to Governor Tim Walz and told him that the

Military is with him all the way. Any difficulty and we will assume control but, when the looting starts, the shooting starts. Thank you!"

In response, Twitter posted a "public interest notice" on the tweet, saying that it violated their policy against glorifying violence. This blocked users from liking, replying, or retweeting the message but left it up and available to view.

Facebook did not remove or label the tweet, which prompted angry responses from users asking why the president was permitted to violate the terms of service while others were not. This incident drew attention to Facebook's established position to protect a particular definition of free expression by allowing harmful rhetoric that amplifies hate speech and threatens civil rights.

In July 2020, Facebook released its civil rights audit. It included input from 100 civil rights organizations. The report concluded that improvements to policies and practices surrounding hate speech detection and removal are still desperately needed. For example, Facebook lacks essential metrics to evaluate the volume of hate speech directed at specific groups.

Should social media organizations seek to more aggressively remove hate speech from their platforms, there are several viable options to pursue based on recent research. To begin, social media organizations could do more to consider context in their removal process. Research in this area suggests that a substantial amount of content that violates existing community standards is not being removed by social media organizations once users have reported it. Providing content moderators with more context should help improve their ability to make more consistent and accurate removal decisions.

Social media organizations should also be more transparent in their efforts to curtail hate speech on their site. Germany's NetzDG law requires social media companies with more than two million users to provide reports regarding what content was reported as hate speech and removed by the company. Expanding these reports to include worldwide removal actions would help individuals, government institutions, and non-governmental organizations to better understand the nature of the problem and develop more comprehensive solutions to address it. Greater efforts at transparency may also help to alleviate concerns that social media organizations are profiting off hate speech posted to their platforms.

Another solution to address the problem of hate speech on social media is for users to simply get off these platforms and instead engage with one another using messaging applications such as WhatsApp or Snapchat. However, the ability to log off assumes a certain amount of privilege on the part of the user. For example, recent college graduates often require social media to secure a job in their chosen field or to stay connected with long-distance family. This approach also gives an enormous amount of power to those who use social media for nefarious purposes, and denies others the benefits of the platforms, such as news-gathering or socializing. In fact, for many members of marginalized groups, such as LGBTQIA youth, social media can provide a way to connect with peers and participate with relevant issues and causes. Simply suggesting that users get off these platforms ignores their benefits and the central role they play in many aspects of life, particularly for young people.

Logging off is not the answer. Instead, public pressure or legal remedies should be considered to motivate social media organizations to invest greater resources into solving this problem. Partnerships between these companies and regulating bodies, such as the European Union or national governments, also seem to be yielding positive results. Regardless of the approach, it is essential that users, regulators, governments, and other institutions remain vigilant in their efforts to minimize the amount of hate speech on social media platforms.

Simply suggesting that users get off these platforms ignores their benefits and the central role they play in many aspects of life, particularly for young people.

FUTURE DIRECTIONS

Hate speech is not a new phenomenon. For centuries, people have been using expression that maligns individuals or groups based on their fixed identity characteristics to maintain their preferred position in a social hierarchy. However, across the globe, hate speech has become less socially acceptable than it was only a few decades ago, even as social media has created a new frontier for hateful rhetoric to exist. In the future, the proliferation or curtailment of hate speech will depend on three primary factors: how it is treated online; how social norms shift regarding free expression and social equality; and how countries and international governing bodies regulate hate speech through legislation.

If social media organizations fail to remove content from their sites, or if governments refuse to hold platforms accountable for hosting extremists, we can expect the volume of online hate speech to continue increasing. Yet, shifting social norms around the laws governing hate speech, free expression, and social equality can also tamp down on the proliferation of hate speech. Already, many cultures do not consider hate speech socially acceptable and prohibit it in public places such as the workplace or in news media. What is also essential in this equation is how people in a particular culture feel about the right to free expression and whether they collectively believe it should be considered more important than the right to human dignity. Shifting attitudes about social equality will also play a role in determining whether and how hate speech is regulated in the future, both politically and socially.

Hate Speech Online

The anonymity provided by many social media platforms or other websites means that individuals can use hate speech online with little fear of offline consequences. In fact, social media platforms such as Gab, 4chan, and 8chan are dedicated to providing unregulated virtual space for those with extreme viewpoints to post racist and anti-Semitic content. Failure on the part of these organizations or the relevant government oversight agencies to address this issue means that hate speech will continue to flourish on these platforms. However, if social media companies and other internet service providers required users to use their real name, the one attached to a government-issued form of identification, it may discourage individuals from creating and disseminating hateful content. At the very least, this would make people accountable for the content they post online.

The primary drawback of requiring people to use their real identities online is the potential chilling effect it would create. Online anonymity allows users to speak truth to power without fear of reprisal. The anonymous release of documents via WikiLeaks is a perfect example of how the promise of anonymity allows information that otherwise may not have seen the light of day to enter the marketplace of ideas. As private companies, each social media organization or Web platform is entitled to make their own decision about whether or not to allow their users to remain anonymous on the site.

Regardless of whether a platform chooses to remove the option of anonymity, employ automatic detection more aggressively, or increase the value placed on human content moderators, some intervention is needed. Without it, online spaces and social media platforms in particular will continue to serve as safe havens for extremists to connect with one another and reinforce their often racist, sexist, or homophobic beliefs. An analysis done by the *New York Times* using data from the Global Terrorism Database, a project of the National Consortium for the Study of

Terrorism and Responses to Terrorism at the University of Maryland, found that since 2011, at least a third of White extremist killers were inspired by others who perpetrated similar attacks.[1] The investigation demonstrated how extremists used social media to connect with one another and reinforce their ideas of racial superiority. In one instance, a school shooter in New Mexico corresponded with a gunman who attacked a mall in Munich. Altogether, they killed 11 people.

The emergence of internet technology, and social media in particular, has coincided with the rise of stochastic terrorism. Also referred to as "lone wolf" terrorism, this phenomenon is defined as the public demonization of a person or group resulting in the incitement of a violent act, which is statistically probable but whose specifics cannot be predicted. According to Juliette Kayyem, former assistant secretary of the Department of Homeland Security and faculty chair of the Homeland Security Program at Harvard University's Kennedy School of Government, there are no lone wolves. In an op-ed for the *Washington Post* following the mass shooting in El Paso in 2019, Kayyem wrote that "viewing what is happening in America today as anything short of an ideological conflict . . . is to disengage each individual incident from the terrorist rhetoric that breeds it."[2]

Kayyem characterizes White supremacist hatred not as a poisonous belief held by isolated individuals, but as a group phenomenon that, according to the FBI, is the greatest terrorist threat to America. White supremacist terror is rooted in mission, kinship, and acceptance, all of which can be found online.

> White-supremacist terrorism has what amounts to a dating app online, putting like-minded individuals together both through mainstream social media platforms and more remote venues, such as 8chan, that exist to foster rage. It is online, much like Islamic terrorism, that white supremacy finds its friends, colleagues who both validate and amplify the rage. When one of them puts the violent rhetoric into action in the real world, the killer is often called a "lone wolf," but they are not alone at all. They gain strength and solace from like-minded individuals. No one would have said an individual Klansman attending a Klan meeting in the woods was a lone wolf; 8chan and other venues are similar meeting spaces in the digital wild.[3]

Demonizing various ethnic groups using social and other forms of media can result in violent acts because the listeners interpret the rhetoric as promoting targeted violence or terrorism. Given that, the value of allowing hate speech on platforms such as 8chan or Gab in the name of protecting free expression is questionable at best. If, instead of White pride propaganda, sites like 8chan and more mainstream platforms such as Twitter were hosting Islamic terrorist propaganda, the content would likely be removed and relevant accounts banned. In fact, Twitter has largely eradicated Islamic State propaganda from its platform but has struggled to do the same with content associated with White nationalism. Although Twitter has not issued an official statement on the matter, company employees who work on machine learning and artificial intelligence have said that the reason Twitter hasn't taken the same aggressive approach to White supremacist content is because the collateral accounts impacted may include those of Republican politicians.[4] As a result of Twitter's inaction, self-professed Nazis, such as former KKK leader David Duke, continue to use the platform to amplify their message of hate.

This is doubly disturbing given the fact that recent research shows that taking down the offending pages or platforms can effectively limit the volume of hate speech online. In 2015, Reddit released a new anti-harassment policy aiming to decrease the amount of "toxic" subreddits notorious for having large amounts of hate speech. After Reddit began removing problematic subreddits, more accounts than expected discontinued using the site, and those that stayed drastically decreased their hate speech usage by at least 80 percent.[5]

Whether it is decreasing anonymity or removing the platforms and pages generating the most extreme content, action (or inaction) on the part of social media companies and other internet service providers will be one of the most important factors shaping the future of hate speech worldwide. However, online communication does not operate in a vacuum. Social norms regarding the use of hate speech, as well as attitudes toward free expression and social equality, will also influence what hate speech looks like in various cultures in the future.

Shifting Social Norms

Only a few decades ago, it was socially acceptable for White Americans to refer to African Americans using the N-word and for Germans to compare Jewish people to vermin. Fortunately, that is no longer the case. Today, there are often negative social consequences for using hate speech. Employers can fire employees for using hate speech in the workplace, and public figures who are caught using hate speech generally (but not always) find themselves ostracized and their popularity diminished.

Attitudes toward the unchecked use of hate speech in places where it is still legally permitted are changing. A 2015 study by the Pew Research Center found that 40 percent of US millennials reported that they were OK with limiting speech that was offensive to minorities, while only 24 percent of baby boomers said the government

Social norms regarding the use of hate speech, as well as attitudes toward free expression and social equality, will influence what hate speech looks like in the future.

should be able to prevent such speech.[6] If this trend continues, these attitudes may continue to progress, and consequently, people may feel less and less comfortable using hate speech. This lack of social acceptance of hate speech and social pressure to restrict its use publicly could lessen its volume and subsequent impact over time.

How people in a given society or culture feel about the right to free expression will also shape the treatment of hate speech in the future. In countries like Germany and Canada, the right to free expression is seen as secondary to an individual's right to dignity. Legal frameworks in these countries reflect this perspective. An individual's right to free expression may be legally curtailed in the name of protecting another's dignity. In Canada, this has meant that offensive jokes by comedians that include hate speech may be punished. In 2016, comedian Mike Ward was ordered by a Quebec Human Rights Tribunal to pay damages to Jeremy Gabriel, who suffers from Treacher Collins syndrome—a condition that affects the development of bones and tissues in the face—for a joke he made about him at a show in 2010. Ward joked that Gabriel, who he assumed had a terminal illness, couldn't be killed even though he'd "tried to drown him once." He also said that when he looked up Gabriel's condition online, he found that it was "being ugly."[7] For some, Ward's punishment feels like justice served. For others, it goes too far and fails to distinguish between speech that incites hatred or violence, and that which is merely offensive. This distinction between illegal hate speech and merely offensive speech is one that countries prohibiting hate speech will have to continue to refine as they seek to balance the right to dignity with citizens' right to free expression.

Another issue that countries restricting the use of hate speech will have to deal with is how to characterize religious beliefs that also meet the legal definition for hate speech. In Canada, hate speech against LBGTQIA folks is defended as being a viable religious belief. The Canadian Criminal Code contains a religious exception, which says that a person may not be convicted for expressing an argument or opinion on a religious subject, or an opinion based on a belief in a religious text. In the future, countries will have to navigate this issue as courts respond to incidents of hate speech that are also expressions of religious opinion, weighing individuals' right to free expression against their right to the free exercise of religion.

In the United States, the right to free expression is revered above all else. The US judiciary has held time and again that the right to free expression is an essential component of democracy that must be protected at all costs. As Chief Justice John Roberts said in *Snyder v. Phelps* (2011), "as a Nation we have chosen a different course—to protect even hurtful speech on public issues to ensure that we do not stifle public debate."[8] However, in her book *The Cult of the Constitution*, legal scholar Mary Anne Franks calls

Americans' staunch commitment to free expression into question. Franks argues that a fundamentalist approach to interpreting the First and Second Amendments, combined with a deregulatory free-market mentality regarding constitutional rights, creates a situation in which the US Constitution works to serve White male supremacy in the United States.[9] In other words, the rights of White males take priority over the rights of others. It is worth noting here that there are categories of expression that the United States chooses not to extend First Amendment protection to, such as obscenity or false advertising. Hate speech simply is not one of them. Yet, as more women and people of color join the US judiciary, it is possible that these attitudes may shift. After all, only two African Americans and four women have served on the US Supreme Court, which has had 114 justices to date.

Along those lines, the extent to which hate speech pervades public discourse in the future will depend greatly upon the social equity in a particular culture or society, and people's attitudes toward it. Social inequity, or perceived social inequity, drives the use of hate speech. An individual may use a derogatory ethnic slur to refer to immigrants in her country because she feels members of that group are threatening her preferred economic, social, and political position. While complete social harmony is likely a utopian idea, the more individuals begin to see people with different identity characteristics as equals, the less likely hate speech is to be widely used. Governments and other institutions can play an important role in this process by establishing hate speech as a category of expression that may be civilly or criminally punished.

Changing Government Regulations

The United Nations encourages all member states to create laws prohibiting incitement to hatred based on race, ethnicity, and other fixed identity characteristics. Despite this, hate speech propagates, particularly online. The way various countries hold social media companies and other service providers responsible for the illegal content posted to their sites will shape the future of how hate speech is created and disseminated. The UN's most recent guidance on this issue, the *Joint Declaration on Freedom of Expression and "Fake News," Disinformation and Propaganda*, strongly restated the position that intermediaries, like Web-hosting platforms or social media sites, should never be held liable for content posted by third parties, unless they specifically intervene in that content or refuse a court order to remove it. However, if social media companies, Web-hosting companies, and other internet service providers are not motivated to address the issue of hate speech on their platforms, it will continue to flourish. Germany and France have both moved to create laws to hold social media companies accountable for illegal hate speech posted to their platforms. Countries that legally prohibit hate speech may want to consider this approach as a way of ensuring that social media and other online platforms are following existing regulations regarding hate speech. In the United States, this debate centers on the protection afforded to internet services by the law colloquially referred to as Section 230. Proponents of free expression fear that if service providers are held liable, it will stifle expression online. As a result, internet platforms are absolved of essentially all responsibility for actions that their users take on their platforms.

While it is unlikely that the United States would move to make all hate speech illegal and thus unprotected by the First Amendment, the door does seem to be opening for civil suits directed at those who spread egregious amounts of online hate. Although the case is likely to be appealed, a woman was recently awarded $14 million in damages for intentional infliction of emotional distress caused by an online personality who called for internet trolls to attack her online.[10] In 2017, Tanya Gersh filed a suit against Andrew Anglin in US District Court for the District of Montana, accusing him of violating her privacy, inflicting emotional distress upon her, and violating Montana's Anti-Intimidation Act. Anglin, who is the founder of the neo-Nazi Web forum the Daily Stormer, published 30 articles instructing his followers to wage a "good old-fashioned troll storm" on Gersh, which resulted in her and her family being targeted by over seven hundred social media posts and phone calls to her home. Many of the messages directed at Gersh, who is Jewish, included slurs and Holocaust imagery. One tweet, directed at Gersh's son, featured an image of an open oven and the message: "*Psst kid, there's a free Xbox One inside this oven.*"

Civil suits like this one provide a pathway for holding those who disseminate harmful hate speech accountable while also addressing concerns about governments restricting free expression. Many scholars rightly cite this fear of government censorship as the reason for allowing hate speech in the United States. It would be better, they argue, to have all expression, including hate speech, out in the open. Otherwise, we run the risk that controversial opinions or information may never see the light of day. Instead, it is best to have all ideas expressed and allowed to compete for acceptance in the speech marketplace.

While the marketplace of ideas should undoubtedly be considered when asking and answering questions about government censorship of speech, it is important to keep in mind that US citizens, and citizens in most countries, do not have equal access to the marketplace, and money can play a large role in determining what information reaches the public sphere. Despite these shortcomings, concerns about the extent to which the government might use a law

Civil suits provide a pathway for holding those who disseminate harmful hate speech accountable while also addressing concerns about governments restricting free expression.

against "hate speech" to silence political dissent must be taken seriously. Given the divisiveness and partisanship that dominates the current US political environment, it is plausible that either party could use a criminal law against hate speech to chill or even punish speech they disagree with. Peaceful dissent is an essential component of any democracy. The possibility that political dissent could be inadvertently suppressed under a potential hate speech regulation is reason enough to avoid federal regulations against hate speech in the United States.

However, there is a substantial and important difference between criminal laws that prohibit hate speech and civil remedies, like those that exist in the United States for intentional infliction of emotional distress and defamation, both of which require a higher standard of proof for public officials and figures, while still giving individual victims of hate speech a form of legal redress. As long as a victim of hate speech is able to prove (1) that there has been extreme and outrageous conduct that is beyond the bounds of decency tolerated in a civilized society, (2) that the conduct caused severe emotional distress, and (3) that the conduct was intentional or reckless, they should be able to bring a successful intentional infliction of emotional distress claim.[11] Civil remedies provide the best path forward for victims of hate speech in the United States. While it does take resources to pursue a legal complaint, this approach keeps the government from being in a position to silence expression, while still providing a form of recourse for those targeted by hate speech.

In the future, legislatures, including the US Congress, should also consider expanding existing defamation statutes to include defamatory statements made about groups based on their fixed identity characteristics, such as race, gender, sexual orientation, etc. While some countries, such as Germany, recognize group defamation, many do not. As Jeremy Waldron successfully argued in *The Harm in Hate Speech,* creating a pathway to sue for the damage hate speech does to one's reputation is an incredibly viable option for victims.[12] Group defamation, along with intentional infliction of emotional distress, both remove the government from the equation, which should assuage justified fears about government suppression of unpopular or dissenting political opinions while still recognizing the harm caused by hate speech.

Conclusion

In the future, the dissemination and impact of hate speech will depend largely on the issues outlined above. How social media companies and other online service providers choose to police hate speech on their platforms will play a substantial role in how hate speech influences individuals and societies worldwide. Social norms around issues such as equality and freedom of expression will determine whether and how hate speech continues to proliferate or recedes. Governments also have the power to shape rules regarding the legality of this expression and determine the punishments, if any, to enact in order to curtail its use.

In order to address the problem of hate speech, each country, institution, and individual must independently decide which of the arguments for and against restricting hate speech they most agree with and which solutions they believe are most feasible. This is not a black and white question. Striking a balance between protecting freedom of expression and respecting human dignity is no easy task. Any approach to addressing the issue requires trade-offs and there are reasonable justifications for censoring hate speech and for protecting it.

One reason to allow hate speech is the desire to have all speech enter the marketplace of ideas, where truth can compete with falsehoods to ensure that truth emerges. In addition, free speech is an essential component of democracy. Citizens need access to information in order to make good decisions about which candidates or policies to support. For many, an individual's personal liberty is reason enough not to curtail their speech, even if it means allowing hateful or hurtful ideas to emerge. Put simply, governments should not be telling people what to think or say. Finally, some see allowing hate speech as a safety valve: a way for people to "let off steam" that stops short of actual physical violence.

Yet, for each of these reasons to protect all expression, including hate speech, there are relevant counterpoints. To begin, there is no empirical evidence to support the notion of a safety valve function being performed by hate speech. Instead, history demonstrates how the widespread use and acceptance of hate speech can create the conditions for incidents of bias-motivated violence and even genocide. Moreover, the speech marketplace of today is largely driven by money and can be manipulated by those with the deepest pockets. There is also such a high volume of speech currently entering the marketplace of ideas that it is hard for citizens to know what is true and what isn't. Disinformation abounds, which raises questions about the role of governments and/or media organizations to help filter what is presented to the public as the "truth."

While a democracy undoubtedly requires free expression, it is not clear what value extremist viewpoints shared by White nationalists on sites like 8chan bring to the political process. Moreover, hate speech can actually work to silence voices in a democracy by prohibiting certain individuals, such as women or people of color, from speaking out on important issues for fear of the hateful responses they are likely to receive. In terms of personal liberty, institutions and individuals must decide what happens when one person's right to free expression infringes on another's dignity. Should the right to human dignity take precedence over the right to free expression?

Any decision to censor hate speech also runs the risk of silencing political dissent or chilling expression. The success of social movements like the fight for civil rights in the 1960s and Black Lives Matter today depends upon organizers' ability to express themselves and their ideas without government interference. However, allowing hate speech can cause psychological and emotional harm to victims and lay the groundwork for bias-motivated violence. It also propagates misinformation in the speech marketplace. For example, when President Trump says that Mexican immigrants are rapists, many people come to believe this lie as the truth. Worse yet, some individuals see this rhetoric as a call to violent action.

In response to this reality, most Western democracies have chosen to put provisions in place that legally prohibit the use of hate speech. There are also countries, such as Japan, where laws discouraging the use of hate speech are on the books but are rarely enforced. Finally, there are those countries, such as South Africa, that have enacted hate speech legislation, only to use it to punish racial minorities from speaking out against their White oppressors.

Each country and culture is bound by its own history and social norms to choose what it sees as the most righteous path. In the United States, this has, for centuries, meant protecting hate speech under the First Amendment.

Stepping back from the legal and technological aspects of this issue, we find moral questions about distinguishing right from wrong.

While that is unlikely to change, there are civil remedies, such as the torts for infliction of emotional distress and defamation, that could be expanded upon or amended in order to give victims of hate speech a legal means of righting the wrong caused by those who seek to malign them based on their fixed identity characteristics.

Stepping back from the legal and technological aspects of this issue, we find moral questions about distinguishing right from wrong. At the end of the day, hate speech is wrong. Even if it's legal, that doesn't make it right. As individuals, we have the capacity to address the problem of hate speech regardless of what our government chooses to do. Particularly for those of us with the privilege to do so, we can and should speak out against hate speech. When we hear it in an off-color joke, when we see it online, or when it is used by those in the public eye to dehumanize an entire group of people, we should condemn it.

ACKNOWLEDGMENTS

Thank you to my husband, Wayne Carlson, for all the things big and small he did to support me throughout this process. From his words of encouragement to his thoughtful edits, I am so grateful to have had him by my side every step of the way.

I also want to thank my parents, Mike and Jackie Ring, my sister Melissa Perricone, my best friend Ben Razes, and my running buddy/boss Chris Paul for always asking me how the book was coming along and for having the patience to listen to my long-winded response to their question.

A big thank-you also goes to my department colleagues and students at Seattle University for their support.

Finally, this project would not have been possible without the guidance I received from my friend and editor Noah Springer at the MIT Press. He believed in me from the beginning and patiently walked me through the entire process (despite my affinity for passive voice). In so many ways, he made this book possible, and for that I am eternally grateful.

Automatic detection
The use of algorithms and/or artificial intelligence on social media platforms to remove content that violates their community standards, both before and after the content has been uploaded.

Content moderation
A series of practices with shared characteristics that are used to screen user-generated content in order to determine what will make it onto, or remain on, a social media platform.

Common law
Legal rules made by judges as they issue rulings on cases.

Community flagging
A process that asks social media users to report content they believe violates the community standards outlined by the company. Reported content is then manually reviewed by employees who determine whether it will be blocked, deleted, or remain on the site.

Community standards
Rules governing what is and is not considered acceptable material to post on social media. Often these regulate not only hate speech but also violence or criminal behavior, bullying, harassment, nudity, sexual solicitation, etc.

Discrimination
The unjust or prejudicial treatment of different categories of people on the grounds of race, ethnicity, national origin, religion, gender, gender identity, sexual orientation, age, or disability.

Expression
The process of making one's thoughts or feelings known. It can include written, verbal, and symbolic forms of communication.

Fighting words
A category of speech identified by the US Supreme Court as exempt from First Amendment protection. Refers specifically to "those personally abusive epithets which, when addressed to the ordinary citizen, are, as a matter of common knowledge, inherently likely to provoke a violent reaction."[1]

Hate speech
Expression that seeks to malign an individual for their immutable characteristics, such as their race, ethnicity, national origin, religion, gender, gender identity, sexual orientation, age, or disability.

Incitement
Broadly, this term refers to the action of provoking someone to unlawful behavior. Within US law, it refers to a category of speech exempt from First Amendment protection. To be considered unprotected, expression must be directed to inciting or producing imminent lawless action and be likely to produce such action.

Marketplace of ideas
This theory holds that in order for truth to be found, all ideas, even bad ones, must be thrown into competition with one another so that the best among them may emerge.

Microaggressions
Verbal, nonverbal, or environmental slights or insults based on discriminatory belief systems that communicate (intentionally or unintentionally) hostile, derogatory, or negative messages about those targeted.

Safe spaces
Designated environments in which students can explore ideas and express themselves in a context with well-understood ground rules for conversations.

Section 230
A section of the Communications Decency Act of 1996 that exempts social media and other internet service providers from liability for what third parties do on their sites. Specifically, it says, "No provider or user of an interactive computer service shall be treated as the publisher or speaker of any information provided by another information content provider."

Speech codes
Rules that prohibit the use of racist or discriminatory comments to demean others based on race, gender, sexual orientation, etc. The Supreme Court determined that hate speech codes created by public universities were too vague and could not be considered a reasonable extension of the fighting words doctrine.

Statutory law
Written law passed by a legislative body.

Terms of service
Private legal contract between a social media company and a user outlining the conditions for use of the service, which the user must agree to in order to access the platform.

Torts
A wrongful act or an infringement of a right (other than under contract) leading to civil legal liability.

Traditional public forum
Places that have been used for assembly, communicating thoughts between citizens, and discussing public questions. Public parks and city sidewalks are both considered traditional public forums.

Trigger warning
Also referred to as a "content warning," this refers to a heads-up given by a speaker or publisher to let the audience know that upcoming material may be upsetting for some.

True threats
Statements where the speaker means to communicate a serious expression of intent to commit an act of unlawful violence to a particular individual or group of individuals. In the United States, true threats are exempt from First Amendment protection and are prohibited by federal law.

NOTES

Chapter 1

1. Abraham Foxman and Christopher Wolf, *Viral Hate: Containing Its Spread on the Internet* (New York: Palgrave Macmillan, 2013), 49.

2. Council Framework Decision 2008/913/JHA on combating certain forms and expressions of racism and xenophobia by means of criminal law (2008), *Official Journal* L328, https://eur-lex.europa.eu/legal-content/EN/TXT/?uri=CELEX%3A32008F0913.

3. Kate Manne, *Down Girl: The Logic of Misogyny* (New York: Oxford University Press, 2018).

4. Alexander Tsesis, "Dignity and Speech: The Regulation of Hate Speech in a Democracy," *Wake Forest Law Review* 44 (May 2009): 505.

5. John Milton, *Complete Poems and Major Prose*, ed. Merritt Hughes (New York: Macmillan, 2003), 719–722.

6. John Stuart Mill, *On Liberty and Other Essays,* ed. John Gray (Oxford: Oxford University Press, 2008), 33.

7. Abrams v. United States, 250 U.S. 616, 630 (1919).

8. Near v. Minnesota, 283 U.S. 697 (1931).

9. Alexander Meiklejohn, *Free Speech and Its Relation to Self-Government* (New York: Harper Brothers, 1948): 13–26.

10. Thomas Emerson, *Toward a General Theory of the First Amendment* (New York: Random House, 1963), 6.

11. Alexander Tsesis, *Destructive Messages: How Hate Speech Paves the Way for Harmful Social Movements* (New York: NYU Press, 2002), 28–65.

12. Ernst Hiemer, *Der Pudelmopsdackelpinscher* (Nuremberg: Der Stürmer-Buchverlag, 1940).

13. William A. Schabas, "Hate Speech in Rwanda: The Road to Genocide," *McGill Law Journal* 46 (2000): 145.

14. David Yanagizawa-Drott, "Propaganda and Conflict: Evidence from the Rwandan Genocide," *The Quarterly Journal of Economics* 129, no. 4 (2014): 1954, https://www.hks.harvard.edu/publications/propaganda-and-conflict-evidence-rwandan-genocide.

15. Mary Kimani, "RTLM: The Medium That Became a Tool for Mass Murder," in *The Media and the Rwandan Genocide*, ed. Allan Thompson (London: Pluto Press, 2007), 112.

16. Scott Straus, "How Many Perpetrators Were There in the Rwandan Genocide? An Estimate," *Journal of Genocide Research* 6, no. 1 (March 2004): 96–98, https://doi.org/10.1080/1462352042000194728.

17. Yanagizawa-Drott, "Propaganda and Conflict," 1950.

18. Steve Stecklow, "Why Facebook is Losing the War on Hate Speech in Myanmar," *Reuters,* August 15, 2018, https://www.reuters.com/investigates/special-report/myanmar-facebook-hate.

19. Adam Leventhal, Junhan Cho, Nareefa Andrabi, and Jessica Barrington-Trimis, "Association of Reported Concern about Increasing Societal Discrimination with Adverse Behavioral Health Outcomes in Late Adolescence," *JAMA Pediatrics* 172, no. 10 (October 2018): 924–933.

20. Laura Leets, "Experiencing Hate Speech: Perceptions and Responses to Anti-Semitism and Antigay Speech," *Journal of Social Issues* 58, no. 2 (2002): 350–358, https://doi.org/10.1111/1540-4560.00264.

21. Mari Matsuda, Charles Lawrence III, Richard Delgado, and Kimberlé Williams Crenshaw, *Words That Wound: Critical Race Theory, Assaultive Speech, and the First Amendment* (New York: Avalon Publishing, 1993), 90–95.

22. Danielle Keats Citron and Helen Norton, "Intermediaries and Hate Speech: Fostering Digital Citizenship for Our Information Age," *Boston University Law Review* 91 (2011): 1447–1452.

23. Danielle Keats Citron, *Hate Crimes in Cyberspace* (Cambridge, MA: Harvard University Press, 2014), 27.

Chapter 2

1. United Nations Human Rights Office of the High Commissioner, Twenty-Second Session, "Rabat Plan of Action," January 11, 2013, https://www.ohchr.org/EN/Issues/FreedomReligion/Pages/RabatPlanOfAction.aspx.

2. UN Human Rights Office, "Rabat Plan of Action."

3. Organization for Security and Co-operation in Europe, "Joint Declaration on Freedom of Expression and 'Fake News,' Disinformation and Propaganda," March 3, 2017, https://www.osce.org/fom/302796.

4. Nazila Ghanea, "The Concept of Racist Hate Speech and Its Evolution over Time," paper presented at the United Nations Committee on the Elimination of Racial Discrimination's Day of Thematic Discussion on Racist Hate Speech, 81st Session (August 28, 2012): 9.

5. Amnesty International, "Written Contribution to the United Nations Committee on the Elimination of Racial Discrimination's Day of Thematic Discussion on Racist Hate Speech, 81st session" (August 28, 2012): 1, https://www.ohchr.org/EN/HRBodies/CERD/Pages/Racisthatespeech.aspx.

6. "Additional Protocol to the Convention on Cybercrime Concerning the Criminalization of Acts of a Racist and Xenophobic Nature Committed through Computer Systems," opened for signature January 28, 2003, *European Treaty Series* no. 189, https://www.coe.int/en/web/conventions/full-list/-/conventions/rms/090000168008160f.

7. German Criminal Code of November 13, 1998, as last amended by Article II of the Act of June 19, 2019, https://www.gesetze-im-internet.de/englisch_stgb/englisch_stgb.html.

8. Whatcott v. Saskatchewan Human Rights Tribunal [2013] 1 S.C.R. 467 (Can.).

9. Tanya Kateri Hernandez, "Hate Speech and the Language of Racism in Latin America: A Lens for Reconsidering Global Hate Speech Restrictions and Legislation Models," *University of Pennsylvania Journal of International Law* 32, no. 3 (2011): 823.

10. Hernandez, "Hate Speech," 828.

11. Marta Rodriguez de Assis Machado, Natália Neris da Silva Santos, and Carolina Cutrupi Ferreira, "Punitive Anti-Racism Laws in Brazil: An Overview of the Enforcement of law by Brazilian Courts," *Section of Law and Democracy of the Brazilian Center of Analysis and Planning* (2015): 10–11, https://www.law.columbia.edu/sites/default/files/microsites/public-research-leadership/marta_macho_-_punitive_anti-racism_laws_in_brazil.pdf.

12. Hernandez, "Hate Speech," 830.

13. Hernandez, "Hate Speech," 830.

14. Alexander Traum, "Contextualizing the Hate Speech Debate: The United States and South Africa," *Comparative and International Law Journal of Southern Africa* 47, no. 1 (2014): 83.

15. Traum, "Contextualizing the Hate Speech Debate," 84.

16. Craig Martin, "Striking the Right Balance: Hate Speech Laws in Japan, the United States and Canada," *Hastings Constitutional Law Quarterly* 45, no. 3 (2018): 464.

17. Koji Higashikawa, "Japan's Hate Speech Laws: Translations of the Osaka City Ordinance and the National Act to Curb Hate Speech in Japan," *Asian-Pacific Law & Policy Journal* 19, no. 1 (2017): 6.

18. Junko Kotani, "Proceed With Caution: Hate Speech Regulation in Japan," *Hastings Constitutional Law Quarterly* 45, no. 3 (2018): 618.

19. Martin, "Striking the Right Balance," 465–469.

20. R.A.V. v. City of St. Paul, 505 U.S. 377 (1992).

21. U.S. v. William White, 810 F.3d 212 (2016).

22. Jeremy Waldron, *The Harm in Hate Speech* (Cambridge, MA: Harvard University Press, 2012), 31–40.

23. Richard Delgado and Jean Stefancic, *Must We Defend Nazis? Hate Speech, Pornography, and the New First Amendment*, reprint edition (New York: NYU Press, 1997), 46.

24. Pew Research Center for Internet and Technology, "Online Harassment 2017 Survey," last modified July 11, 2017, http://www.pewinternet.org/2017/07/11/online-harassment-2017.

25. Steven Lukes and Andrew Skull, *Durkheim and the Law*, 2nd ed. (London: Palgrave Macmillan, 2013), 78–102.

Chapter 3

1. Mike Hayes, Albert Samaha, and Talal Ansari, "Imagine Being Surrounded by People Who Hate You and Want to See You Dead," *Buzzfeed News*, September 27, 2017, https://www.buzzfeednews.com/article/mikehayes/we-found-154-incidents-of-college-hate-speech-and-violence.

2. Papish v. Board of Curators of the University of Missouri, 410 U.S. 667 (1973).

3. Board of Regents of the University of Wisconsin System v. Southworth, 529 U.S. 217 (2000).

4. Doe v. University of Michigan, 721 F. Supp. 852 (E.D. Mich. 1989); The UWM Post, Inc. v. Board of Regents of the University of Wisconsin System, 774 F. Supp. 1163 (E.D. Wis. 1991).

5. Erwin Chemerinsky and Howard Gillman, *Free Speech on Campus* (New Haven, Connecticut: Yale University Press, 2018), 97–103.

6. Henry Louis Gates Jr., Anthony Griffin, Donald Lively, Robert Post, William Rubenstein, and Nadine Strossen, *Speaking of Race, Speaking of Sex: Hate Speech, Civil Rights, and Civil Liberties* (New York, NYU Press, 1994), 45.

7. Tatro v. University of Minnesota, 816 N.W.2d 509 (Minn. 2012).

8. Oyama v. University of Hawaii, 813 F. 3d 850 (2015).

9. Alexander Tsesis, "Campus Speech and Harassment," *Minnesota Law Review* 101 (2017): 1901.

10. University of Idaho, Student Code of Conduct: Article II, https://www.webpages.uidaho.edu/fsh/2300.html; University of Wisconsin, Code of Conduct, https://www.wisconsin.edu/regents/policies/discrimination-harassment-and-retaliation; University of California–Berkeley, Student Code of Conduct, https://sa.berkeley.edu/code-of-conduct.

11. Barack Obama, "Remarks by the President at Town Hall on College Access and Affordability" (speech, Des Moines, Iowa, September 14, 2015), https://

obamawhitehouse.archives.gov/the-press-office/2015/09/15/remarks-president
-town-hall-college-access-and-affordability.

12. Greg Lukianoff and Jonathan Haidt, *The Coddling of the American Mind:
How Good Intentions and Bad Ideas are Setting Up a Generation for Failure* (New
York: Penguin Books, 2018), 28–35.

13. Nadine Strossen, *Hate: Why We Should Resist It with Free Speech, Not Censorship* (New York: Oxford University Press, 2018), 34.

14. Jacob Poushter, "40% of Millennials OK with Limiting Speech Offensive to Minorities," *Pew Research Center*, November 20, 2015, http://www
.pewresearch.org/fact-tank/2015/11/20/40-of-millennials-ok-with-limiting
-speech-offensive-to-minorities.

15. Alexander Tsesis, "Burning Crosses on Campus: University Hate Speech
Codes," *Connecticut Law Review* 43, no: 2 (2010): 665.

16. College Pulse and Knight Foundation, *Free Expression on College Campuses*
(Miami, Florida: John S. and James L. Knight Foundation, 2019), https://
www.knightfoundation.org/reports/free-expression-college-campuses.

17. Matal v. Tam, 137 S. Ct. 1744 (2017).

18. Richard Delgado and Jean Stefancic, "Four Ironies of Campus Climate,"
Minnesota Law Review 101 (2017): 1927–1928.

19. Diana Ali, *Safe Spaces and Brave Spaces: Historical Context and Recommendations for Student Affairs Professionals* (Washington, DC: National Association of
Student Personnel Administrators, 2017), 1.

20. John Palfrey, *Safe Spaces, Brave Spaces: Diversity and Free Expression in Education* (Cambridge, MA: MIT Press, 2017), 15–16.

21. Ali, *Safe Spaces*, 3–4.

Chapter 4

1. Pew Research Center for Internet and Technology, "Online Harassment
2017 Survey," last modified July 11, 2017, http://www.pewinternet.org/
2017/07/11/online-harassment-2017.

2. Johan Farkas, Jannick Schou, and Christina Neumayer, "Cloaked Facebook
Pages: Exploring Fake Islamic Propaganda in Social Media," *New Media & Society* 20, no. 5 (2018): 1856–1865.

3. Jesse Daniels, "Race and Racism in Internet Studies: A Review and Critique," *New Media & Society* 15, no. 5 (2013): 695–719.

4. Mari Matsuda, Charles Lawrence III, Richard Delgado and Kimberlé Williams Crenshaw, *Words That Wound: Critical Race Theory, Assaultive Speech, and
the First Amendment* (New York: Avalon Publishing, 1993), 26.

5. Matsuda, *Words That Wound*, 90–95.

6. Danielle Keats Citron and Helen Norton, "Intermediaries and Hate Speech: Fostering Digital Citizenship for Our Information Age," *Boston University Law Review* 91, (2011): 1447–1452.

7. Danielle Keats Citron, *Hate Crimes in Cyberspace* (Cambridge, MA: Harvard University Press, 2014), 27.

8. "Countering Illegal Hate Speech Online: EU Code of Conduct Ensures Swift Response," European Commission press release, February 4, 2019, http://europa.eu/rapid/press-release_IP-19-805_en.htm.

9. Tarleton Gillespie, *Custodians of the Internet: Platforms, Content Moderation, and the Hidden Decisions That Shape Social Media* (New Haven and London: Yale University Press, 2018), 78.

10. Gillespie, *Custodians of the Internet*, 78–82.

11. Jessica Pater, Moon Kim, Elizabeth Mynatt, and Casey Fiesler, "Characterizations of Online Harassment: Comparing Policies across Social Media Platforms," *Proceedings of the 2017 ACM Conference on Computer Supported Cooperative Work and Social Computing* (2017): 1501–1513.

12. Zach Beauchamp, "Milo Yiannopoulos's Collapse Shows That No-Platforming Can Work," *Vox*, https://www.vox.com/policy-and-politics/2018/12/5/18125507/milo-yiannopoulos-debt-no-platform.

13. Thomas Davidson, Dana Warmsley, Michael Macy, and Ingmar Weber, "Automated Hate Speech Detection and the Problem of Offensive Language," in *Proceedings of the Eleventh International AAAI Conference on Web and Social Media* (Montreal, Canada, May 15–18, 2017): 1, https://aaai.org/ocs/index.php/ICWSM/ICWSM17/paper/view/15665.

14. Safiya Noble, *Algorithms of Oppression* (New York: NYU Press, 2018).

15. Catherine Buni and Soraya Chemaly, "The Secret Rules of the Internet: The Murky History of Moderation and How It's Shaping the Future of Free Speech," *The Verge*, April 13, 2016, https://www.theverge.com/2016/4/13/11387934/internet-moderator-history-youtube-facebook-reddit-censorship-free-speech.

16. Kate Klonick, "The New Governors: The People, Rules, and Processes Governing Online Speech," *Harvard Law Review* 131, (2018): 1640.

17. Casey Newton, "The Trauma Floor: The Secret Lives of Facebook Moderators in America," *The Verge*, February 25, 2019, https://www.theverge.com/2019/2/25/18229714/cognizant-facebook-content-moderator-interviews-trauma-working-conditions-arizona.

18. Kurt Wagner, "Facebook Is Building an Oversight Board. Can That Fix Its Problems?" *Bloomberg News*, June 24, 2019, https://www.bloomberg.com/news/articles/2019-06-24/facebook-is-building-an-oversight-board-can-that-fix-its-problems.

19. Sarah Myers West, "Censored, Suspended, Shadowbanned: User Interpretations of Content Moderation on Social Media Platforms," *New Media & Society* 20, no. 11 (2018): 4372.

20. Leona Yi-Fan Su, Michael Xenos, Kathleen Rose, Christopher Wirz, Dietram Scheufele, and Dominique Brossar, "Comparing Patterns of Incivility in Comments on the Facebook Pages of News Outlets," *New Media & Society* 20, no. 10 (2018): 3698–3692.

21. Caitlin Ring Carlson and Hayley Rousselle, "Report and Repeat: Investigating Facebook's Hate Speech Removal Process," *First Monday* 25, no. 1 (2020): 17–28.

Chapter 5

1. Weiyi Cai and Simone Landon, "Attacks by White Extremists Are Growing: So Are Their Connections," *New York Times*, April 3, 2019, https://www.nytimes.com/interactive/2019/04/03/world/white-extremist terrorism -christchurch.html.

2. Juliette Kayyem, "There Are No Lone Wolves," *Washington Post,* August 4, 2019, https://www.washingtonpost.com/opinions/2019/08/04/there-are -no-lone-wolves.

3. Kayyem, "No Lone Wolves."

4. Joseph Cox and Jason Koebler, "Why Won't Twitter Treat White Supremacy like ISIS? Because It Would Mean Banning Some Republican Politicians Too," *Vice News,* April 25 2019, https://www.vice.com/en_us/article/a3xgq5/ why-wont-twitter-treat-white-supremacy-like-isis-because-it-would-mean -banning-some-republican-politicians-too.

5. Eshwar Chandrasekharan, Umashanthi Pavalanathan, Anirudh Srinivasan, Adam Glynn, Jacob Eisenstein, and Eric Gilbert, "You Can't Stay Here: The Efficacy of Reddit's 2015 Ban Examined through Hate Speech," *Proceedings of the ACM on Human-Computer Interaction* 1, no. 2 (2017): 10–17, https://doi .org/10.1145/3134666.

6. Jacob Poushter, "40% of Millennials OK with Limiting Speech Offensive to Minorities," *Pew Research Center*, November 20, 2015, http://www .pewresearch.org/fact-tank/2015/11/20/40-of-millennials-ok-with-limiting -speech-offensive-to-minorities.

7. Tamara Khandaker, "A Comedian Was Ordered to Pay $42,000 Because He Insulted a Child with a Disability," *Vice News*, July 21, 2016, https://www .vice.com/en_us/article/wjaykq/a-canadian-comedian-was-ordered-to-pay-42000 -because-he-insulted-a-child-with-a-disability.

8. Snyder v. Phelps, 562 U.S. 443 (2011).

9. Mary Anne Franks, *Cult of the Constitution* (Stanford, CA: Stanford University Press, 2019).

10. Gersh v. Anglin, 353 F. Supp. 3d 958 (D. Mont. 2018).

11. Restatement (Second) of Torts § 46 (1965).

12. Jeremy Waldron, *The Harm in Hate Speech* (Cambridge, MA: Harvard University Press, 2012), 31–40.

Glossary

1. Chaplinsky v. New Hampshire, 315 U.S. 568, 571-72 (1942).

FURTHER READING

Baer, Ulrich. *What Snowflakes Get Right: Free Speech, Truth, and Equality on Campus*. New York: Oxford University Press, 2019.

Chemerinsky, Erwin, and Howard Gillman. *Free Speech on Campus*. New Haven, CT: Yale University Press, 2018.

Citron, Danielle Keats. *Hate Crimes in Cyberspace*. Cambridge, MA: Harvard University Press, 2014.

Delgado, Richard, and Jean Stefancic. *Must We Defend Nazis? Hate Speech, Pornography, and the New First Amendment*. Reprint edition. New York: NYU Press, 2018.

Fish, Stanley. *The First: How to Think about Hate Speech, Campus Speech, Religious Speech, Fake News, Post-Truth, and Donald Trump*. New York: Atria/One Signal Publishers, 2019.

Foxman, Abraham, and Christopher Wolf. *Viral Hate: Containing Its Spread on the Internet*. New York: Palgrave Macmillan, 2013.

Gillespie, Tarleton. *Custodians of the Internet: Platforms, Content Moderation, and the Hidden Decisions That Shape Social Media*. New Haven, CT: Yale University Press, 2018.

Herz, Michael Eric, and Peter Molnar, eds. *The Content and Context of Hate Speech: Rethinking Regulation and Responses*. Cambridge, UK: Cambridge University Press, 2012.

Manne, Kate. *Down Girl: The Logic of Misogyny*. New York: Oxford University Press, 2018.

Matsuda, Mari, Charles Lawrence III, Richard Delgado, and Kimberlé Williams Crenshaw. *Words That Wound: Critical Race Theory, Assaultive Speech, and the First Amendment*. New York: Avalon Publishing, 1993.

Noble, Safiya. *Algorithms of Oppression*. New York: NYU Press, 2018.

Palfrey, John. *Safe Spaces, Brave Spaces: Diversity and Free Expression in Education*. Cambridge, MA: MIT Press, 2017.

Roberts, Sarah. *Behind the Screen: Content Moderation in the Shadows of Social Media*. New Haven, CT: Yale University Press, 2019.

Stone, Geoffrey, and Lee Bollinger, eds. *The Free Speech Century*. New York: Oxford University Press, 2018.

Strossen, Nadine. *Hate: Why We Should Resist It with Free Speech, Not Censorship*. New York: Oxford University Press, 2018.

Tsesis, Alexander. *Destructive Messages: How Hate Speech Paves the Way for Harmful Social Movements*. New York: NYU Press, 2002.

Waldron, Jeremy. *The Harm in Hate Speech*. Cambridge, MA: Harvard University Press, 2012.

INDEX

The MIT Press Essential Knowledge Series

CAITLIN RING CARLSON is an Associate Professor in the Communication Department at Seattle University. Her research focuses on media law, policy, and ethics from a feminist perspective. She lives in Seattle with her husband, Wayne, and their dog, Rocco.